# Longevity in Leadership

*How to Run the Race and Finish Well*

Bruce Lindley

"Longevity in Leadership - How to Run the Race and Finish Well" by Bruce Lindley

Copyright © 2023 Bruce Lindley

Published by ARC Global PO Box 3398, Helensvale B.C. QLD 4212, Australia

This book or parts thereof may not be reproduced in any form, stored in a retrieval system, or transmitted in any form by any means – electronic, mechanical, photocopy, recording or otherwise – without prior written permission of the publisher, except as provided by Australian copyright law.

Unless otherwise noted, quotations are taken from the Scriptures taken from the Holy Bible, New International Version®, NIV®. Copyright © 1973, 1978, 1984, 2011 by Biblica, Inc.™ Used by permission of Zondervan. All rights reserved worldwide. The "NIV" and "New International Version" are trademarks registered in the United States Patent and Trademark Office by Biblica, Inc.™

Scripture quotations marked (NASB) taken from the NEWAMERICAN STANDARD BIBLE®, Copyright ©1960, 1962, 1963, 1968, 1971, 1972, 1973, 1975, 1977, 1995 by The Lockman Foundation. Used by permission.

All Scripture quotations marked (TPT) are from The Passion Translation®.

Copyright © 2017, 2018, 2020 by Passion & Fire Ministries, Inc. Used by permission. All rights reserved. ThePassionTranslation.com

Scripture quotations marked (NLT) taken from Holy Bible. New Living Translation Copyright© 1996, 2004, 2007, 2013 by Tyndale House Foundation. Used by permission of Tyndale House Publishers Inc., Carol Stream, Illinois 60188. All rights reserved.

Scripture quotations marked (NKJV) taken from the New King James Version®. Copyright © 1982 by Thomas Nelson. Used by permission. All rights reserved.

ISBN: 978-0-6450498-1-7

Printed in Australia

# Dedication

Longevity in Leadership – How to Run the Race and Finish Well is dedicated to all the amazing leaders who have led by example in life. And most importantly, to our Lord Jesus Christ who is the best example of a leader to follow!

This is also dedicated to my precious wife Cheryl, whom I have the honor of running the race of life with for Jesus.

I especially dedicate this book to the remarkable apostles and prophets in our amazing apostolic community ARC Global. What an honor it is to run the race and complete the course of life and ministry with you. We get to equip, mentor, and raise up leaders for the Kingdom of God together.

# Acknowledgements

This book wouldn't have been possible without the support and help of my amazing wife Cheryl Lindley and our wonderful Apostolic Restore Community (ARC) Global family. Thank you.

Special thanks to Pamela Segneri for her wonderful editing skills. And to the amazing Paul Segneri for his practical contribution to the publishing of this book and to our ministry. We love you both.

# Endorsements

*My good friend Bruce Lindley has released a Spirit-inspired book that will equip generations and activate them to fulfill the biblical call—to run with endurance the race that is set before us (Hebrews 12:1). No matter your age or current stage of life, this book is for you. Take this message to heart, and by God's grace, run with it!*

*Dr. Ché Ahn, Senior Leader*
*Harvest Rock Church, Pasadena, CA*
*President, Harvest International Ministry*

*I have known Bruce and his lovely family for about 20 years. His integrity, passion for Jesus, love for people, and humility back up the wisdom in this book. Having known hundreds of leaders over the past 40 plus years of ministry, Bruce amazes me with his buoyancy and capacity to thrive in difficult situations. I've seen him in his happy place and seen him carrying the crushing weight of organizational dysfunction. True to himself, he has become a father* to many. I am not surprised that he has written this practical, easy to read book on leadership. It will help you upgrade from "surviving" to thriving!

> Dr. Charles Stock, Senior leader
> Life Center Ministries International
> Founder, Clear River Apostolic Network
> Harrisburg, Pennsylvania USA

I really enjoyed the wisdom in this wonderful book. Covering important subjects such as intimacy, spiritual disciplines and raising up the next generation, Bruce shares keys that he has learned that have proven fruit today. I highly recommend Longevity in Leadership – How to Run the Race and Finish Well to all in leadership. If you prayerfully and intentionally apply these principles to your life, you can also experience longevity, joy and fruitfulness in ministry.

> Katherine Ruonala, Senior Leader
> Glory City Church Brisbane Australia
> Co- Founder, Glory City Network

At a time when the media is bombarding us with the failure of Christian leaders, Bruce's latest book is an outstanding blueprint on Christian leadership birthed out of both; the very real challenges Bruce has walked through following God's *calling in radical obedience and having mentored many Kingdom leaders. The book deals with the disciplines needed for "success in ministry" and the keys to longevity in life and ministry. Longevity in Leadership – How to Run the Race and Finish Well is essential reading for all Christian leaders and emerging leaders.*

Peter Dunstan, Co-Founder<br>
Breakfree Australia

*Kedemah in the Hebrew language speaks of leadership. It means to "go forward, to advance or in the modern dialect: "let's go!" It is the word of a commander leading his troops into battle. Bruce's heart in writing Longevity in Leadership – How to Run the Race and Finish Well is to teach the next generation the principles and practices of godly leadership, as well as encourage the present. Through this book, he imparts the Father God's vision of governance, then urging them to "run with it." Bruce Lindley's words will strengthen your faith, guide you, encourage you and help you finish victorious in the race of God's high calling for your life.*

Gene Little, Director<br>
Global Outpouring House of Peace, Jerusalem

*When I read a book, I ask if the author really lives what they write. I can assure you, after nearly 15 years running together, Bruce has been a fantastic finisher. I have witnessed his commitment to discovering and chasing his destiny and his main passion to see others fulfill theirs. This hunger is accompanied by a desire to live a life of integrity and balance. This book will help you align all these aspects and more.*

*Dr. Mark D. Tubbs, Founder*
*Transformation of the Nations*

# ENDORSEMENTS

# Contents

Introduction .................................................... 15

Part 1 - The Challenge ................................... 23
    1. Growing Concern Of Leaders Not Finishing Well
    2. God's Destiny For Your Life
    3. What God Requires Of You
    4. God Perspective For Longevity In Leadership
    5. Learn How To Run The Race
    6. Make Your Leadership A Spacious Place

Part 2 - How to Finish Well ........................... 85
    1. Overcoming Challenges In You
    2. Dealing With Obstacles And Discouragement
    3. Being Able To Re-Vision
    4. Intimacy With The Father
    5. Change To Kingdom Values
    6. New Spiritual Disciplines

Part 3 - Your Leadership Timeline ................. 159
    1. The Phases Of Leadership Development
    2. The Generalised Timeline
    3. Your Leadership Timeline

Part 4 - Your Next Generation Legacy ........... 185
    1. Your Ceiling Their Floor
    2. Success With A Successor
    3. Your Next Generation Legacy
    4. It's Your Turn Now

Final Word – You Will Finish Well ................ 211

End Notes ...................................................... 219

# Introduction

As somebody who was a long-distance runner when I was young, I have always loved watching long distance races. The most famous long-distance race of course is the Olympic marathon. We had the privilege of visiting the historic Olympic Stadium in Athens, Greece. It has a very different shape to most running tracks today. It's more oblong than round. Most importantly it is the home of the first modern Olympic Games in 1896.

Greece is also the place where the first recorded marathon was run. Marathon is a town in Greece. But the first marathon there was not a race.

In 490 BC Philippides, a courier, or a day runner, ran to share the news of the victory that had been won in the battle of Marathon. He ran 42 kilometres (26 miles) to the battlefield near Marathon and back to Athens to announce the Greek victory over Persia. When he arrived back in Athens he declared, "Joy to you, we've won" and then collapsed and died.[1]

Some of my most powerful memories of the modern Olympic marathon events over the years are runners who are near the finish of the marathon. Sadly, as some run into the stadium after nearly completing 42 kilometres, you see that they are in trouble. They still need to run the final 500 metres inside the stadium. It's so confronting and tragic to see them collapse on the track before they reached the finish line. They had run so far, but they weren't able to finish the race.

While this is all very fascinating, the analogy for leaders is very powerful.

If you are a leader, you understand the significance of your need to run the marathon of your life and ministry well.

When I was a young Christian, at 19 years of age, we were experiencing the global phenomenon in the body of Christ. It was called the Charismatic Renewal. It was different from the Pentecostal movement because it involved traditional churches experiencing the power and baptism of the Holy Spirit for the first time on a global scale. It began in an Episcopalian church in Van Nuys California and a Catholic seminary in Pennsylvania in the mid 1960s and swept through traditional denominations worldwide for two decades. It was characterised by scripture in song worship, emphasis on the baptism of Holy Spirit, and people praying for healing of others. Members of the congregation were allowed to flow spontaneously in the gifts of the Holy Spirit during the church services for the first time and there was

## INTRODUCTION

great joy and freedom in worship. For traditional churches that were used to hymns and conservative meetings this was a radical change.

Our little Methodist Church exploded. From a handful of elderly people to an inflow of young people, especially university students who were passionate for Jesus. We thought that this was normal Christianity until one day I received a phone call in the church office from another evangelical church in our city.

She said -

*We hear that you are having revival there.*

My response was -

*Are we?*

We thought this was the normal Christian experience.

Our Sunday night church services were overflowing with young people full of the joy of the Lord. My future wife, Cheryl, was a university student at that time and she had a small cargo van with no seats in the back. She would go around her campus asking who would like to come to church. She never had a problem filling it with students. Nobody minded sitting on the floor of the van. Everybody was excited to go because God was there.

I remember one night where there was the normal explosion of joy in worship, the worship leader at the end of one song said, 'turn to the person beside you and rejoice with them'. Across the aisle from me was the father of the pastor's wife.

His name was Lance Lithgow.

He was so full of the joy of the Lord that he was still dancing and jumping for joy between the formal church pews even though the singing had stopped. After we greeted each other, I asked him how old he was? He said he was 94 years old.

At 94 he was full of the Holy Spirit, zeal, and health. He had been a Christian since he was teenager. I was amazed and inspired by his passion and longevity of zeal for 80 or so years.

Here in front of me was an example of a Christian leader with longevity and finishing well.

Out my mouth came these words-

*I am going to be just like you at 94!*

At that moment I knew I would be full of the joy of the Lord and still on fire and radical for Jesus at 94. More importantly I would be influencing, equipping, and raising up the next generation to do the same thing.

Interestingly Lance's daughter, Leonie, is now 91. She truly is her father's daughter. His example has been reproduced into

## INTRODUCTION

the next generation through her and her sister. To this day, she is full of the zeal of God and authority. She still challenges me to run my race to finish well. Even more importantly, all her children and grandchildren all love God and are involved in leadership in the Kingdom of God.

Longevity is something that we all want, but most of us don't know how to get it, let alone live it.

It is much more than living to an old age in good health.

Leading with longevity is leading with the zeal of God all your life and raising up the next generation to do the same for future generations.

As you read, I believe God will help you step into longevity in your leadership, ministry and you will learn to finish well.

This book has been a long time coming. It was not because I've lacked motivation to write it.

My own leadership formation and convergence was not at a place that would impact and transform your leadership development. For you to transform others' lives, you first must be transformed.

This is a leadership book with a difference. It won't just inspire you. It will equip and help you to run your race and finish well. It will also help you understand that generations are dependent on you today. They are waiting for you to look beyond your immediate ministry and see that you need to help this next generation to begin to run their leadership race well too.

In Psalms 78, God gives His legacy challenge to you. He desires that your leadership will impact your own future generations. Not just for them to love God but for them to carry the next generation leadership mandate to equip and impact their future descendants too.

Asaph the Psalmist decreed in Psalms 78:5b-7(TPT)

> ...he commanded our forefathers to teach them to their children. For perpetuity God's ways will be passed down from one generation to the next, even to those not yet born. In this way, every generation will set its hope in God...

I have good news for you. You are about to be equipped for longevity in your leadership and to finish your race well. Generations are waiting for you.

My prayer is that the Holy Spirit will transform you so that your leadership style will change dramatically so you will truly have longevity and next generational legacy.

## INTRODUCTION

This book is also a workbook and your opportunity to respond and grow.

At the end of each chapter, a workbook page is included. Use the following to summarise your key points, list the things that you need to change and a time to implement them:

| Action Points | My Response | Date |
|---|---|---|

Are you ready?

# Part 1 – The Challenge

# 1. Growing Concern Of Leaders Not Finishing Well

Cheryl and I were at a national conference recently. It was wonderful to see so many of our friends all in one place together after three years of Covid which had prevented those from different states in Australia travelling and gathering.

While it was a joyful reunion, I was however concerned for a few ministry couples who either had major health issues or were discouraged because of key leaders leaving and many of their congregation not coming back after the Covid restrictions were lifted. I was concerned for them because they were overtired, overwhelmed, and just worn out.

Sadly, they are not alone! There are so many discouraged, sick, weary leaders who are beaten up by their circumstances, health issues, marriages under strain and just worn out. More and more come to the end of themselves and then stop! Many resign and many even leave the ministry. Some stop going to church altogether and even backslide.

This is all in addition to the regular media headlines of famous pastors failing morally, lacking some sort of integrity, and even acting illegally.

What started as a trickle has now become a torrent!

But this is not how God wants us to lead and to live!

God wants us to finish well!

When I was 10 years old, I was invited to join an athletics club in my suburb. I enjoyed competing weekly during the athletic season as I was quite a good runner. Towards the end of the season, we joined with other clubs in the region for the athletic carnival. After competing in many sprint races, high jump, and long jump, I had done well over the entire day.

Then they announced that it was time for the final event of the day. The 1500 metre race. I had never heard of it before. So, I asked how many laps of the track 1500 metres was. I was told it was four laps. I remember thinking,

*No problem, I can do that.*

However, once the race started and I completed one lap sprinting, I discovered that there was a problem! I had started my race too fast and had not paced myself. I was running slower and slower as the race progressed. So much so that by the third lap I was walking. I was not alone. Other competitors were also walking and some even dropped out of the race.

I learned a very important lesson that day! You must pace

## PART 1 - THE CHALLENGE

yourself!

It's not just about competing in a long-distance race but more importantly in life and leadership.

Yes, life, leadership and ministry are not a 100 metre Sprint… it's a marathon!

But even more importantly… It is not HOW you START. It is HOW you FINISH!

When I meet leaders around the world, the first question that I ask is, 'Are you enjoying your ministry?'

Most of them look at me with a puzzled look on their face.

Enjoy ministry?

They had never considered that.

They always thought that leadership and ministry had to be endured rather than being enjoyed!

As a young man at university before I became a Christian, I was searching for meaning in life. I bought a poster for my bedroom wall that said, 'Life is a journey, not a place.' Even though I didn't truly comprehend what it meant, I knew deep in my heart that it was true.

Why? Something deep inside of us longs for the ability to

enjoy the journey of life. In this way we do not just achieve goals, but build a successful career, find a lifelong partner in marriage or even pursue fame and fortune.

The truth is that you will not have longevity in leadership and ministry if you don't learn how to pace yourself. And if you don't enjoy the journey, you won't have longevity and finish well.

Even more importantly you won't have next generational legacy.

The good news is that there is a way to experience all these things for God's glory and for you finish well.

| Action Points | My Response | Date |

## 2. God's Destiny For Your Life

First and foremost, you need to know God's destiny for your life!

However, I have discovered that most Christians are unable to articulate what is God's specific plan for their life.

When my daughter and her husband where young leaders in the church that we used to lead, they responded to an altar call one Sunday. Asked why they had come forward for prayer, they replied-

*We want to know God's plan for our future.*

As I began to pray for them, I heard God say-

*Tell them they are called to into the ministry.*

But I wasn't prepared for their immediate reply of an emphatic Nooooo!

The reason was obvious. My daughter had grown up in this church planting pastor's home and she had seen the hardship, pain, disappointment and rejection we had gone through for years. The last thing she wanted was to be a pastor of a church.

Fast forward 14 years and they are the senior associate pastors of their church.

They had discovered and grown into God's call for their lives and are living it today.

How do you know God's plan for you with clarity?

**1. The most important realization is that you and I were created for a purpose.**

*Psalms 139:16 All the days (of your life) were written in the book before one of them came to be!*

You were created for a divine purpose.

The true meaning in life is all about you living your God purpose.

*Jeremiah 29:11 "For I know the plans I have for you," declares the Lord, "plans to prosper you and not to harm you, plans to give you hope and a future."*

The definition of a fulfilled life is 'finding your God given destiny from God & living it.'

It is called a destiny!

There is no expiry date on your divine purpose. It's never too late to begin.

There is no 'Use By' date on your destiny.

It is not just any destiny! God has created you for a DIVINE destiny!

**2. God has created each one of us for a divine purpose.**

It is very important to discover your destiny but it's only the first step.

To live your destiny, you must do something.

You can't expect God to do it for you.

Most leaders can precisely articulate their God destiny.

However, if you are unable to do that, here is the best way to discover God's destiny for your life.

Take some time to meditate and answer this question.

If you had unlimited time, finances, and opportunity what would you do for the Kingdom of God?

Passion is a powerful force. Once you bring your desires and passion under the lordship of Christ and seek his will for your life and not your own will. Then you'll discover your God destiny quickly.

So, take 10 or 15 minutes right now and begin to dream the God dream. Ask yourself that question, 'What would I do for God if I had unlimited time, finances and opportunity'?

If you could do anything for Him, what would it be?

Begin to meditate and pray over it the next few days. You will find it will become a lot clearer.

**3. Each of us must 'position ourselves' in God's divine purpose for our life.**

Yes. It is God's plan for your life, but it won't just happen. You're not going to wake up one day and your divine purpose has been fulfilled.

It is conditional and it is still your choice. You must choose to obey God and partake in His destiny for your life.

I hear so many Christians saying things like-

*If it is meant to be it will just happen.*

That is not Christianity!

*It will ALL work out in the end.*

No, it doesn't. You must do something!

*I'm just trusting God ...*

No, you are not. Because you need to put your call into action.

The worst one that is said is-

*All things work together for good.*

That is one of the most misquoted scriptures in the Bible. Why? Because they are quoting only half the verse.

The rest of Romans 8:28 says-

*To those who have been CALLED according to HIS purpose.*

So, you have to respond to the call of God on your life to live your specific 'God purpose'.

To do that you must decide to live God's plan for your life above every other plan that you might have.

**4. To fulfil your God destiny, you need to do something.**

Sometimes fulfilling your destiny requires great change. And you must be bold to bring about that change.

For others it means having the courage to do the thing that you have always been passionate about. Often it means changing careers and even moving geographically.

Change is uncomfortable and it is costly.

But I've learnt that it is better to choose to change than being forced to change.

Change into God's destiny produces right fruit and fulfillment for your life and family.

**5. Make sure you do it God's way.**

I've seen many Christians be presumptuous and decide they know the best way to fulfill God's destiny for their lives. So instead of receiving wise counsel and mentoring from mature and wise leaders, they presume they know best and rush ahead with disastrous results.

One of the worst examples of not doing it God's way is the story of Joseph in Genesis 37-50.

In Genesis 37 Joseph did have God's dream of divine purpose but he made wrong choices.

Why? Because he was Immature and didn't know how to interpret it.

He made the classic mistakes. He was not wise because he didn't have any discernment.

The main reason was he was not fathered properly.

Joseph's father Jacob spoiled and loved him more than his brothers. This is not the way to raise a child.

The result was that Joseph was so immature that he nearly destroyed his destiny.

So, Joseph had to do it the hard way.

It took slavery and prison to mentor him to be ready to step into his God purpose.

He had to deal with pride and remove the 'coat of self' off his life. That coat he was given by his father never was a dream coat. It became a 'coat of self-promotion' and a stumbling block. Self-promotion never results in you filling your destiny and achieving your life goals.

Joseph's father's favouritism and unwise gift was a stumbling block for Joseph. It potentially destroyed God's divine purpose for him and Israel.

The good news is that Joseph finally did fulfill God's destiny for his life.

After years of pain and hardship we read that God promoted him from the prison to the palace and he becomes ruler over Egypt second only in authority to Pharoah. As we read the account, his brothers do indeed bow down to him when they come to buy food amid the famine.

In Genesis 45:3, Joseph finally reveals who he is to his brothers-

> *I am Joseph! Is my father still living? But his brothers were not able to answer him because they were terrified at his presence.*

However, Joseph was not angry or bitter.

Why? Joseph finally saw God's big plan and his divine purpose became a reality.

He finally understood that God was using him to fulfil God's destiny for Israel.

> *Do not be distressed and do not be angry with yourselves for selling me…*

> *Because it was to save lives that God sent me ahead of you.*

> *God sent me ahead of you to preserve for you a remnant on earth and to save our lives by a great*

> *deliverance...It was not you who sent me here but God!*

God always has a bigger picture.

The answer is to say 'Yes' and to be patient. I have learned that God is not in a hurry. Learn to find God in the process.

Learn to stand back until you see clearly and discover God's timing. If you are too close, you won't see the big picture or God's timing and you will attempt to fulfil your destiny prematurely.

Finally, by way of the false accusation and wrong imprisonment, Joseph addressed the failures in his life.

He dealt with his pride.

He dealt with his self-promotion.

He dealt with his prison and victim thinking.

Amid his hardship Joseph had a choice. It would either break him or make him.

He decided to allow the false accusation and wrong imprisonment to make him.

Why? Because he had chosen Gods way, the favor of God came on him. He ended up fulfilling God's plan for his life.

So will you! Just like Joseph, your call depends on you!

Jeremiah 29:12-13 says-

> *Then you will call on me and come and pray to me,*
> *and I will listen to you.*
> *You will seek me and find me when you seek me with*
> *all your heart.*

You are also created for a divine purpose. God desires that you discover and fulfil that purpose.

God says in Jeremiah 29:14 that if you do that you will be-

*Found by God.*

This means God will help you discover and step into living your God destiny.

The main prayer that I pray for those in my circle of influence who aren't living for God is,

*Lord bring them back into alignment with their God destiny.*

Why? Then it's not what you think they should be. Instead it will help align their lives with God's destiny. We cannot expect God to force people to do something against their will.

However, we can pray that God will align them with their God destiny.

We have seen this prayer answered multiple times. It works!

Why? Because God wants you to discover your destiny in life and live it.

PART 1 - THE CHALLENGE

**Action Points** | **My Response** | **Date**

## 3. What God Requires Of You

What does God require of you once you discover your God destiny?

The most important thing you can do is to decide to fulfil God's destiny for your life.
It's the most exciting and fulfilling way to live.

Why? You are fulfilling the reason why you were created.

I often say to my wife Cheryl,
> *How awesome is this? We get to live God's destiny for our lives.*

As soon as I became a Christian at 18 years of age I was on fire for God. I knew I was called into full time ministry. I had an accountancy decree and working as a graduate in an accountancy practice, but I was miserable.

Even though it was a secure career, I knew I was created for something greater. I was called into the ministry.

Over the years as a pastor and a leader in our city, I've been offered other job careers. I was once asked to enter local politics in my city. But my answer has always been the same-

*I have a higher calling on my life.*

I have met so many Christians that are frustrated, unfulfilled and even miserable because they are working in a career that they were never meant to be in. Others have chosen to chase wealth and success over God's call, but the result is always the same.

In Exodus 3:5-7 we learn how not to answer God's call.

Moses had what I call "But God" disease. Every time God told him to do something he had an excuse.

His first excuse in verse 11 was-

*Who am I?*

In other words, he didn't know who he was.

In leadership development this is called the Identity Challenge. You need to know who you are in Him.

But Moses goes from bad to worse.

In verse 13, Moses argued that he did not know what to say.

God always has the answer-

*Tell them I am sent you.*

God promises to give us the words to speak.

PART 1 - THE CHALLENGE

Psalms 81:10 says that if we-

*Open our mouths he will fill it.*

Moses next excuse was in Exodus 4:1–

*What if they don't believe me or listen to me?*

But that wasn't Moses' concern. His only requirement was to obey God and God would do the rest.

Then he argued in verse 10-

*But I can't speak.*

Fear will always shut your mouth and shut you down.

If you are afraid to speak up or speak publicly, go and get deliverance.

Jesus who is perfect love casts out all fear. God will set you free and fill you with his Holy boldness.

Moses last excuse was the ultimate rejection of his God destiny for his life.

In Exodus 4:13, Moses said-

*Pardon your servant Lord. Please send somebody else.*

In other words-

*No! I'm not going to do it.*

However, the outcome was not good. It goes on to say that-

*God burned with anger.*

And he chose Aaron to speak for him instead!

The truth is your destiny is conditional!
It is dependent on your submission and obedience to Him.

The good news is that Moses and Aaron did finally obey God! You don't need to go through all of this to get to that place. Why don't you decide right now and pray-

*Yes, Lord I'm willing to obey your destiny for my life.*

Nations are dependent on your obedience to the call of God.
In 1989, the traditional domination that we were in insisted that I needed to go to seminary for more training. So, our young family obeyed God and left Australia and moved to Los Angeles in the USA. I thought it was for me to study Church growth and leadership at Fuller seminary.

After we decided to go, I discovered that Cheryl was pregnant with our fourth child. In my immaturity and naivety I said,

*No problem, we'll just wait until the baby is born then go.*

PART 1 - THE CHALLENGE

When our daughter Sarah was three weeks old, we sold everything and left Australia.

We didn't know what lay ahead of us, but we obeyed God & moved to the USA. That set off a chain of events of substantial hardship of no permanent place to live for six-months that would have been averted had I waited for another six months before going there. Even though I got the timing wrong, in the midst of our pain God led us to a local church in Pasadena that had been planted by Che Ahn and Lou Engle.

Decades later Che Ahn is still our spiritual father. I became Lou Engle's prayer partner when I was in the church there for four years. Years later in 2004 back in Australia we led 'The Call', a National Day of Prayer and fasting with thousands of young people that turned our nation powerfully in a single day.

Years later two of our daughters as teenagers returned to the USA, to participate in an internship with Lou in the Justice House of Prayer in Washington DC. That prayer movement along with many others, helped overturn the legalisation of abortion, Roe v Wade decades later. It set a fire in our daughters' hearts.

We thought God was leading us to the USA for a specific reason, but he had a much larger plan for us.

Yes, it was our destiny. But God had a much bigger plan. He

also used it to catapult our children into their destiny.

Decades later all our five children are on fire for God.

Our youngest daughter, Sarah, is an emerging next generation prophet who has an expanding ministry. She is a great preacher and moves powerfully in the Holy Spirit. I am excited to say that she will easily surpass all that I have achieved.

Do you see now why it is so important to obey God's destiny for your life?

Generations are dependent on your obedience.

PART 1 - THE CHALLENGE

**Action Points** | **My Response** | **Date**

## 4. God's Perspective For Longevity In Leadership

Paul the apostle was and still is the best example of longevity and devotion in the New Testament.

In 2 Timothy 4:7 he said-

> *I have fought the good fight, I have finished the race, I have kept the faith.*

In 2022, my wife and I travelled to Italy for the first time to see our extended family who live there.

We had a few days to visit Rome on the way home. While it was interesting to see the more famous locations, my wife Cheryl continued to encourage me to find Paul and Peter's jail cell where they were imprisoned before they were martyred. We found it. Near the Roman Forum is the small ancient Mamertine Prison. It was where Paul wrote the book of Second Timothy.

As we descended steps into the prison dungeon, it took my breath away. So much so that I had to sit down on the steps. I couldn't move for a long time. I was overcome by the cost of being an apostle of Christ. Not only was the jail cell in darkness it also was cold and damp in the middle of summer.

Paul was imprisoned there for over a year. We saw the holes in the wall where the prisoner's chains were fixed and there was a small round shelf that would hold a lamp.

Not only was I moved by the price that he paid for the sake of the gospel, but also impacted by the weight of his amazing words that he had written in 2 Timothy 4:7.

He indeed had "fought the good fight" and "kept the faith."
But what impacted me the most, was that he had finished his race right where I sat.
More than that, he had finished his race well!

In Philippians 3:12b-14 Paul urges us to imitate him-

> *I press on to take hold of that for which Christ Jesus took hold of me. Brothers and sisters, I do not consider myself yet to have taken hold of it. But one thing I do: Forgetting what is behind and straining toward what is ahead, I press on toward the goal to win the prize for which God has called me heavenward in Christ Jesus.*

And then he adds in verse 15 for our benefit.

*All of us, then, who are mature should take such a view of things.*

There is a 'press' that is required.

We need a holy determination to press on to fulfill our own call of God no matter what.

The writer in Hebrews 12:1 puts it this way-

> *Therefore, since we are surrounded by such a great cloud of witnesses, let us throw off everything that hinders and the sin that so easily entangles. And let us run with perseverance the race marked out for us…*

There are some important keys here for us to finish well.

First Paul says to-

> *FIX and KEEP FIXING our eyes on Jesus.*

I've heard Bill Johnson speak about his prayer life. He says that if it is a long time or even a few minutes to pray, he will spend three quarters of that time in worship.

Why? Because he practices keeping his eyes fixed on Jesus. This is a great challenge to us all.

Worship causes you to look at the face of Jesus, so we are

'fixated' on Him, and not on the circumstances of our daily world.

We must fix our eyes on Jesus first before we can know him as the-

*AUTHOR and FINISHER of OUR FAITH.*

Faith rises out of intimacy and devotion with Jesus.
And faith requires daily exercise.
As one of my good friends says-

*You must cross the 'God is good' bridge every day!*

This is the starting point for fixing our eyes on Jesus and building our faith. He alone is your source.
As you worship and pray you will build your 'inner man', so you become strong and consistent.

As well as worship and prayer, we need to bathe in the word of God every day.

In Ephesians 5:26 Paul calls it by the-

*Washing of water through the word.*

Years ago, when we used to witness on the streets, people would often accuse us of being brainwashed. I always took it as a compliment not an accusation. I would say in reply 'Thank you'.

And would go on to say 'my brains were unclean, and they needed to be washed by the word of God'.

In other words, you need to wash your mind every day with God's word.

I'll talk more about how to do that effectively later in the section on spiritual disciplines.

When we spend time every day in worship and in God's word and when we pray in the Holy Spirit, we then receive encouragement and victory and refreshing from the Holy Spirit.

Paul says it this way in 1 Corinthians 14:4-

*Anyone who speaks in a tongue edifies themselves.*

In other words, we build ourselves up and encourage ourselves in Him!

Refreshing comes from his presence and through 'our helper' the Holy Spirit.

Then we able to agree with Paul in Hebrews 12:1 and

*Run with perseverance…*

Most preachers emphasise 'the race' rather than the 'perseverance'.

But perseverance is essential to finishing well!
So, we will talk more about how to persevere in the next section.

Perseverance[2] is the-

*Continued effort to do or achieve something despite difficulties, failure, or opposition.*

Not just enduring with gritted teeth. I used to be like that. I thought that perseverance was just hanging on for grim life. But I had no understanding of what it was to truly 'stand firm' (Ephesians 6:14).

The truth was I wasn't standing in faith at all. I was just refusing to give up. Even though I was commendable when I was battered and bruised, that was not perseverance. No that was stubbornness. Jesus was not glorified.

True perseverance comes when the spirit of victory is attached. It is when you refuse to be a victim and feel sorry for yourself. Instead, you live in the spirit of victory regardless of your circumstances.

When you have true perseverance, you are victor not a victim!

More importantly you learn how to overcome your circumstances and opposition no matter what.

This is what it means to be an 'overcomer'.

As you overcome with perseverance, you increase in authority and maturity.

This is what the Bible calls 'steadfastness'.

| Action Points | My Response | Date |
| --- | --- | --- |

## 5. Learn How to Run the Race

Most long-distance runners know how to find a rhythm when they run. You must learn to find your rhythm in God.

When you pace yourself when you are running, everything seems to be in balance and complementary.

You find the perfect pace when your breathing, fitness level, energy, and speed all converge together. This is often called "running within yourself". In other words, you know that if you go too fast you won't be able to run as long however if you keep up the balanced pace you can go longer and far further than you thought was even possible.

**To run the race, you need to know how to pace yourself.**

James 1:12 says-

> *Blessed is the one who perseveres under trial because, having stood the test, that person will receive the crown of life that the Lord has promised to those who love him.*

In contrast, if we don't finish well then not only is our life affected but also our many other spheres of influence.

One of the saddest examples is to see Prince Harry lashing out in the media at his family and anyone else he disagrees with. Even when family members have apologised to Prince Harry, he cannot forgive them. Princess Kate apologised over a minor incident with their daughter's flower girl dress the day before Princess Megan's wedding and even sent flowers and a written apology. But both Prince Harry and his wife were not able to forgive and let go of any offence.

Why? Because Harry has never dealt with the trauma of losing his mother Princess Diana when he was eleven years old.

As I was praying about this, I saw a vision of a topographical map. An earthquake had just taken place in the middle of the map, and there were multiple shock waves in concentric circles going out from the traumatic event. I realised that this was how Prince Harry was living. Sadly, the increasing shock waves will continue to isolate him from those he loves, instead of helping him.

Whether your trauma is caused by your actions or the actions of others, if you don't deal with that incident and subsequent trauma, it will follow you all your life.

We all will experience hardship in life. It seems to be even more intense when you step into fulltime ministry.

In fact, it often feels like God uses opposition and pain to build our character and leadership gift.

So, the answer is not to give up. And to allow God to build perseverance and longevity into your life. And you will learn how to finish well.

In Proverbs 4:26-27, King Solomon explains it this way-

> *Give careful thought to the power for your feet and be steadfast in all your ways.*
> *Do not turn to the right or to the left keep your foot from evil.*

Here is the solution. Note the Progression.

Conviction-> Humility-> Repentance of Offence and Sin-> Forgiven-> Restoration.

The problem is most people in life ignore that inner prompting of guilt. They don't respond to God's prompting to deal with their sin or that they're wrong. If you ignore that inner voice of your conscience long enough it will stop speaking to you. Your heart will just get harder.

The answer is to respond to that conviction God's way.

It takes honesty, self-awareness, and humility to admit that you were wrong, and you need to ask forgiveness. Both to God and to another person.

But if you not only respond in humility and then repent of your sin, it says in James 4:6 NKJV

> *God resists the proud but gives grace to the humble.*

God's promise is clear in 1 John 1:9

> *If we confess our sin God is faithful and just to forgive our sin and cleanse us from all unrighteousness.*

God's word is true. If you repent in humility in response to God's conviction of your sin, He will forgive you.

It's a wonderful thing to know that you have been forgiven.

What happens next is more wonderful. Not only are you forgiven but He restores you!

Even though you don't deserve it God says "Not guilty" when we are repentant.

In Luke 15 is Jesus' story of the prodigal son returning to the outstretched arms of his father.
Verse 21 tells us how the son repented.

> *Father, I have sinned against heaven and in your sight..."*

He goes on to say,

> "I am no longer worthy to be called your son".

The father's response to his son's humility and repentance was love and total restoration.

Verse 22-24 tells us the father said to his servants in response to his son coming home.

> "Quick! Bring the best robe and put it on him. Put a ring on his finger and sandals on his feet. Bring the fattened calf and kill it. Let's have a feast and celebrate. For this son of mine was dead and is alive again. He was lost and (now he) is found".

God responds in the same way to you and I when we truly repent. There is a celebration in heaven.

He not only forgives us, He 'restores our soul'.

This is the true Christian lifestyle. God's word says we are supposed to live this way. If you don't, you won't fulfil our destiny.

**Run with Perseverance**

New Christians are often surprised that after they repent of their sin and give their lives to Jesus and accept Christ's forgiveness, they often expect life to be bliss from there on.

The reverse is true. So many declare they had more problems after they were Christian than they did before they became a Christian.

Why is that so? The answer is you weren't a threat to evil in your selfish, sinful lifestyle. You were doing a good job being self-centred. But when you become a Christian, you automatically become a threat. In fact, you've just gone to war.

John Wimber[3] paints this picture that will help you understand.

> *"Most new Christians think that their life will be a cruise after they come to Christ. They go down to the dock thinking that they're going to get on a cruise ship and cruise throughout the rest of their life. but when they arrive at the dock the ship is not painted white it is painted grey. They are not boarding a cruise ship but a warship!"*

It is not God who sends the hardship. You have an enemy of your soul.

The good news is that according to Romans 8:31

> *If God is for us, who can be against us.*

God is on your side. Jesus has already won the victory. You need to step into it.

We do need His help to walk through obstacles in life and leadership and grow strong through it.

The good news is that when you repent of your sins, Not only are you cleansed, but you are also set free.

Freedom comes in your soul and God begins the process of restoration.

As Peter decreed in Acts 3:19 (NKJV)

> *Repent therefore and be converted, that your sins may be blotted out, so that times of refreshing may come from the presence of the Lord...*

Not only does He forgive you, but also, He restores you. Then you will develop great perseverance and you will enjoy the steadfast journey of life.

**How to Persevere**

Perseverance means you do not give up no matter what happens. Quitting should not be in your vocabulary.

In Ephesians 6 talks about the spiritual warfare every believer experiences. Ephesians 6:10 says

> *Be strong in the Lord and his mighty power.*
> *Yes, you must decide to be strong!*

But the good news is you're not doing it in your strength. You now have the capacity to be strong in His mighty power.

In verses 14–17, Paul instructs us to put on the whole armour of God.

> *Why? So, you can take your stand against the devil's assignments against you.*

One of the pieces of your armour is the shield of faith.
In verse 16 Paul says you must-

> *Take up the shield of faith.*

Recently I heard a friend in ministry preaching on our need as leaders to do this every day. She shared a recent experience of how she was approached by a woman at the altar of the church after she finished preaching. Even though it had been a very powerful church service and the ministry had touched a lot of people's lives, the woman was critical and abusive.

My friend was stunned. Walking away she said to the Father-

> *What was that?*

She heard the Father reply-

*That was push back.*

He went on to say-

*Where was your shield of faith?*

She said she had forgotten to put up her shield of faith. This spoke loudly to me as it has happened to me as well. It is often in the least likely situations where God has moved powerfully and His presence is still lingering, there will be an attack against you.

Paul says in verse 16, the shield of faith will-

*extinguish all the flaming arrows of the evil one.*

You must make sure that you intentionally put up your shield of faith each day. Especially when you are walking into a ministry and a potentially difficult situation.

The other area that the devil attacks us is through our own mind. That is why Paul says in verse 17 we are to

*take the helmet of salvation.*

The battle for the mind is the greatest battle that you'll ever face.

The Bible says that we need to have the mind of Christ!

That is why it's so important to do what Paul says in Romans 12:2-

> *Do not conform to the pattern of this world but be transformed by the renewing of your mind. Then you will be able to test and approve what God's will is..."*

In other words, you will be able to do God's will and fulfil your God destiny.

Earlier in Ephesians 5:26 Paul says that we need to renew our minds-

> *with the washing of the water by the word.*

The Word of God is the key to renewing your mind. This is why you need to wash in the Word of God every day.

Make it a spiritual discipline. I have learnt that when you make the word a discipline, it will soon become a delight. You will love doing it every day.

Don't just read a verse of the day or someone else's devotional, I use a daily bible reading plan that enables me to read through the entire Bible in one year. Not only is it a great spiritual discipline it is also a great blessing.

## PART 1 - THE CHALLENGE

Every day I sense God speaking to me and refreshing me and even recalibrating and renewing my mindsets to His perspective. It has become one of the great joys of my life.

Paul says in Ephesians 6:17 that the word of God is-

> *the sword of the spirit.*

Not only should you read the word of God, but also speak God's word out of your mouth.

When you speak out God's promises in faith and decree his word, Job 22:28 NKJV tells us-

> *Declare (decree) a thing and it will be the established for you......So light will shine on your ways.*

Breakthrough and victory come when you put on the whole armour of God. Get the Word of God IN you. Use the sword of the word to shift opposition, circumstances and opposing powers of darkness.

You will begin to live in victory and not always under so much attack.

This is one of the ways to begin to step into longevity in your leadership.

| Action Points | My Response | Date |

## 6. Make Your Leadership A Spacious Place

When we're facing tough times, God has a way through your circumstances and every obstacle that you will face.

The best example of this is David when he was running for his life from King Saul.

In Psalms 31 we read that David was under acute pressure and facing death.

In the midst of all this pain, he has a revelation from God that-

Verse 8 says-

*You have set my feet in a spacious place.*

The word spacious is normally used to describe and open space or a large house.

but there is an even more specific definition –

Larger in extent or capacity than the average…

What does a 'spacious place" look like?

My wife Cheryl often talks about needing to go out of the city into the country or to the beach, so she has room to breathe - but that's not what a true spacious place is.

A spacious place is not a tree change or a physical place. It is a place of deep encounter with God.

You thrive when this takes place. When you thrive you are healthy, and strong, you will always do well, flourish, increase.

To live in a spacious place is more than a positive perspective and an optimistic outlook on life.

It means that you can live a life of passionate faith with peace. When you're in a spacious place you are creative. The Bible teaches us that we are made up of three parts - body soul and spirit.

It is in your spirit that Jesus lives and where your conscience dwells. It is also where creativity comes from. You are grounded and at peace regardless of what is taking place in your life.

When you live this way, you are content, patient, grateful and blessed.

You have an inner peace which overflows onto others.

When David declared that God had set him in a spacious place, he was saying that he had blessed him with a great capacity to cope and conquer in the most difficult circumstance.

We all have hardship. Sometimes it doesn't just last a short time! Saul was pursuing and attempting to kill David for many years. Despite all the fear and stress David stepped into a spacious place in God.

How do we walk through times like that and still live in a spacious place?

Psalms 84:4 gives us the answer-

*Blessed are those who dwell in your house, they are ever praising you.*
*Blessed are those whose strength is in you, whose hearts are set on pilgrimage.*

We don't use the word pilgrimage much in western society these days.

Our ministry is connected to a House of Prayer in Jerusalem. We take teams on prayer assignments each year. We have learned that the easiest way to pass through passport control and border security in Tel Aviv is to say that we are entering Israel on 'pilgrimage'. Pilgrims have been going to Israel for over 2000 years.

But what is the true meaning of the word pilgrimage?

Webster's dictionary[4] says a 'pilgrimage' is best defined as-

*A person's journey through life, including personal growth. It involves a spiritual focus or pathway which leads you to an encounter with God".*

Normally we don't expect an encounter or growing closer to Jesus, to involve acute hardship.

**Power in the wilderness**

In Mark 1:9-11 Jesus had a wonderful experience at his baptism.

Heaven opened and the Holy Spirit fell on him. He heard the Father tell him that he was His beloved son. He would have felt very blessed.

But look at what happens next!

Mark 1:12 says-

*At once the Spirit sent him out into the wilderness....*

What just happened?

God had just blessed him remarkably but why did he have to go into the wilderness?

PART 1 - THE CHALLENGE

We have a problem with our western secular thinking. We don't equate 'blessing' with 'wilderness' experiences, problems, and acute pain. I do believe that God is good, and He blesses his children. But that blessing is not always ease and freedom from pain in life.

Wilderness was part of God's will for Jesus. And it will often be His will for us.
It wasn't just for a few days. It was for 40 days.
He wasn't camping and singing songs of worship around a campfire.
No! He was being tempted by Satan for 40 days.

Recently I broke my left hand and then a few months later broke my left shoulder. This was after surgery on that same shoulder three months before.

If you didn't know that Jesus had been led by God into the wilderness to be tempted by Satan and I told you that God had blessed me over those months, most would say "that doesn't sound like God to me".

Why? Because we have no grid for it!
But the wilderness is where Jesus grew in great power.

In Luke 4:13-14 it says

> *When the devil had finished all this tempting, he left him ....*

And

> *Jesus returned to Galilee in the power of the Spirit....*

How did that happen?

The answer is what David discovered in Psalms 84:6.

It says David learnt to

> *.... **pass through** the valley of Baca.*

The valley of Baca was well known in David's days. It literally meant "the place of weeping".

A place of weeping is a place of hardship and requires great endurance.

Most Christians would say, "I never want to visit there..." and "that is not on my wish list!"

But you're missing the point!

You 'pass through' the valley of weeping. You don't live there!

David not only caught this truth he lived it. That's why he said in Psalms 23:4 NKJV

> *even though I **walk through** the valley of the shadow*

*of death...*

David understood that you are only meant to pass through hardship and pain including the valley of death, but you were never meant to live there!

**A Place of Springs**

If you're able to embrace this process, then something important happens when you are there.

You learn to do what David did in Psalms 84:6.
You will make your hardship and pain-

*...a place of springs*

How do you make a place of hardship a place of springs?

Simple answer is you press into God when everything goes wrong. You don't run away from him. You run to him.

Here's some practical ideas that will help transform your valley of weeping into a place of springs-

- Worship. The Internet is a gift to the body of Christ. You can have worship playing for hours, even 24/7. In the process you learn to truly rejoice in the Lord always.
- Speaking in tongues more and more every day.
- Encourage yourself in the word of God.

- Read the great revivalists of Christian history.
- Declare the promises of God out loud. And make sure that you...
- Decree the following-

  *I am a victor not a victim and God is doing a good work in me. I will come out of this with even more power of the Holy Spirit.*

When you do these things, you will turn your place of weeping into a place of springs. Springs are where living water flows!

This is what it means to live the victorious Christian life.

This is what it means to live in a spacious place.

It is what leaders do. You turn hardship into a place of springs, a place of encounter with God, a place of breakthrough and blessing.

So regardless of your present situation - how difficult or easy, how challenging or restful life maybe right now, God wants you to live in a spacious place.

Once we say yes to this lifestyle of living in a spacious place, God fills you with the power of His Holy Spirit to overcome and persevere.

**As your days are so your strength will be.**

Many years ago, during a time of prayer I decided that I was never going to retire.

I heard the Lord say,

> Do not retire, instead refire.

I knew exactly what the Lord meant. He was telling me that ministry is a life lifelong calling.

And if I say yes to that call, then he would give me longevity.

So, every time somebody asks me when I'm going to retire, I always say-

> I am not retiring. I am refiring.

There is no retirement age to your call of God. You are not subject to a denomination or a church board or other people's opinions. You can keep going as long as God gives you strength. Praise God.

In Deuteronomy 33 Moses decrees in verse 25 NKJV

> As your days, so shall your strength be.

God's word has many layers of context. That's one of the things that I love about the word of God.

Not only does it speak and its original context, but it also speaks to our lives today.

When God gave his people a promise in the Bible, we can expect that same promise as his son or daughter today.

So, when Moses promises Asher in Deuteronomy 33:25 NKJV

*As your days are so your strength will be.*

We can also receive that promise of longevity.

It is not just a promise to live a long time. Now it's more than that!

The promise of longevity of years is also longevity of your ministry and your leadership.

The context is that earlier in Deuteronomy 32, Moses was giving his final blessing to Israel before His death. So in Chapter 33 he blesses them. He blesses each of the twelve tribes, one at a time.

Over each one he decreed their strength and prophesied their future.

In verse 24 Moses blesses Asher. He decrees-

*Asher is the most blessed of all sons.*

He goes on to decree –

> *Let Him be FAVOURED by His brothers (emphasis mine)*

Then he gives the powerful analogy-

> *Let him DIP his foot in OIL.*

In other words, 'Let Asher be anointed for His future'.

In verse 25 NKJV he goes on-

> *The bolts of your GATES shall be iron & bronze.*

Other Bible versions replace the word 'gates' with 'shoes.'

What was Moses saying? He was saying to Asher that God will give him strength, maturity, authority, and influence'.

He will do the same for you.

**You need to learn how to live in this.**

The older I become the more I understand the power of this principle.

God has always intended that His sons and daughters live their whole lives in authority and in victory. Not to limp or fall over the finish line. But to finish our race running with strength and power.

This blessing and this promise of - 'As your days are so your strength will be', still speaks to us today.

It is your decision. Do you want longevity in your leadership?
God's promise is true, and it is yours. Believe and receive it and it will become your reality.

Like my pastor's father, the promise is also for you to live all your life healthy and strong.

This is a great promise of long effective healthy Spirit filled leadership. All the days of our lives.

Is that possible?
Yes! If you believe it and go after it in faith. It will be yours.

PART 2 – HOW TO FINISH WELL

**Action Points** | **My Response** | **Date**

# Part 2 – How To Finish Well

## How Do You Finish Well?

Paul the apostle said this in Hebrews 12:2, for all believers -

*Fix your eyes on Jesus…*

You must be single minded in your determination to fulfil the call of God over your life.

Often when I prepare to speak to emerging apostles, prophets and leaders, I see a vision of us as thoroughbred racehorses in a life-long race. It's a picture of my calling. I see that my racehorse has blinkers on his eyes which makes the horse only look forward. He's unable to be distracted by what's happening beside him. His sole focus is the finishing post before him.

I believe Paul had a similar picture in mind when he said you must fix your eyes on Jesus.

How can I be so sure?

Hebrews 12:2 goes on to say if we do, He is–

*The author and FINISHER of our faith!*

He not only causes you and enables you to begin this race of ministry and leadership, but he also gives you the grace to finish that race well.

However, finishing well doesn't just happen.

It's not a case of being at the right place at the right time. No, it's just the opposite.

To finish well, you must be intentionally willing to embrace change as well as pursuing greater dimensions of your relationship with God.

## 1. Overcoming Challenges In You

A leader must deal with many major challenges the longer you stay in ministry. I am not just talking about not committing adultery or lack of financial integrity. The book of Proverbs says that these things will destroy you as well as your family and so many Christians in your immediate sphere of influence. All I can say is that if you struggle with any of these things get professional help with ongoing accountability before you begin your leadership journey.

But there are other issues that need to be dealt with for you to have longevity as a leader.

It has been my experience and observation that you must cross the bridge and deal with pride and selfish ambition. Most leaders may not talk about it openly but every one of us has had to deal with that at some stage in our ministry. Numbers, numbers, numbers! But success is not about the size of your ministry. It is the size of your influence.

I've also lost track of how many leaders have sacrificed their family on the altar of ministry. One of the key issues that a leader must face is how to balance family with your ministry.

We have had the blessing of being mentored powerfully in this by our long-time pastors, Che and Sue Ahn. We learned that it was not about the size of our ministry, but how well our marriage and family is doing that defines success in ministry. This is such a high value that at our leadership meetings we will always ask accountability questions concerning how we were travelling in a marriage relationship.

Do you have a day off each week that prioritises your marriage and children? When I was young in ministry my day off was all about mowing the lawn, cleaning the house, doing laundry, and going grocery shopping. It was very unusual to stop and spend quality time with my wife and family all day. In fact, the kids were normally at school on my day off. All that gradually changed as we were taught how to prioritise family night, family devotions each day, date night with our spouse and praying together in agreement every day.

Another important challenge in ministry that needs to be overcome is learning how to deal with stress and discouragement. Stress can be overcome through encountering God's peace and learning how to have a daily peace operating system.

Often, it's a learned reaction that must be systematically unlearned by applying the promises of God's word through meditation and confession but most importantly through intimacy with God the Father.

The truth is that you must learn to live in the Spirit 'under pressure'.

But you still need to make lifestyle changes in several key areas.

**1. Marriage**

Building your marriage must be the main priority in your ministry It is also the enemy's main assignment against your ministry. 1 Timothy 3 says that it will either qualify you or disqualify you.

So, it is important to build a healthy marriage.

Here are some the keys-

You need to pray with your spouse every day.

There is power in the statement-

*Those that pray together, stay together.*

As a young leader sure I knew the importance of personal prayer time, but I had never considered praying with my wife each day as well.

The first and most important way to pray together is The Prayer of Agreement.

The prayer of agreement saved our marriage. We spend 5

to 10 minutes today praying specifically for our marriage, extended family, health, finances and over things God has told us to do.

Matthew 18:19 says-

*If two of you on earth agree about anything they ask for it will be done for them by my Father in heaven.*

We try to have communion together each day. We seal our prayers of agreement with the seal of communion - the blood and body of Jesus.

Make sure you have a set time set aside for each other each week. We call it our weekly date. You can go for a walk on the beach or even go out for a meal together. The main objective is for you to both communicate with each other. So, it can't involve going to the movies or watching TV. Put away your screens. Talk to each other. Listen to each other. Communicate.

**2. Family**

Your next priority must be your children no matter how old they are.

As my spiritual father Che says,

*The truth is you never stop being responsible for your*

*children.*

My experience is that this is not only true but extremely important, especially if your adult children are not walking with Jesus.

One of the greatest challenges for parents who are pastors is that their adult children often fall away from God. God is giving me great compassion for Christian leaders who are in this situation. I always make sure I pray with them and agree that God will bring home the prodigal sons and daughters.

### 3. Raising Godly Children

Foundations are the most important thing to build when you're building a home. it is the same for raising children.

We prioritised praying with each child each night before they went to sleep. We had five children. Yes, that took us a long time each night. Cheryl started with the youngest and I started with the oldest. It would take over an hour each night. But we were committed to our children knowing that they were loved by God and loved by us. One of the keys was we didn't stop doing that as they got older.

As they became teenagers, we discovered the longer we sat there the more they talked to us.

This good communication resulted in none of the children

rebelling or backsliding or wanting to leave home as prodigals.

We chose to home school our children as it fitted so well with our ministry lifestyle. We were in the United States for four years when our children were very little and there were not many other safe options. We had a great support network through the home school movement. When they were much older, they did go to Christian high school where they blossomed.

Now all our children are on fire for God. Two of them are in the ministry. All four of our daughters are prophets and part of an amazing prophetic church.

Because they all flow so powerfully in the prophetic, the main question that our adult children are asked by young Christian parents is

> *How did your parents teach you to hear the voice of God?*

Their answer is always the same.

> *We were taught how to hear God's voice at a very young age. As we became older, we knew how to listen to God's direction for everyday living.*

If they ever had a problem, we would always ask them-

> *What does God say about that?*

If they said, 'I don't know' then we would tell them to go into their bedroom and ask Jesus, 'What do you want me to do?' or 'What is your solution, Lord?'

They learnt to hear the voice of God.

So much so they began to return quickly to tell us what they heard.

Our normal response was 'that sounds like God to me'.

When our children were teenagers, we encouraged them not to date but to go out with their group of friends instead. Our girls decided that they were going to keep themselves for their future husbands until their wedding day. All our children understood the need to marry a Christian spouse. They saw the power of this in us, their parents, as we prayed, worshiped, and lived the Kingdom of God together in our family.

Our church was a street level church. As a result, we attracted a lot of young people who were either from broken families whose parents were absent or addicts. Often, they had been abused and had resorted to drinking, drugs and partying with all sorts of painful results.

Our children saw this firsthand. We discipled a number of newly saved homeless teens by having them live with us.

Without realising it we drug proofed and discipled our

children. When they turned 18 they didn't rebel, back slide or choose the night club party lifestyle that was tempting to so many Christian teens in our city. They had seen the destructive results of that lifestyle firsthand and didn't want to have any part of it for themselves.

On a more positive note, we also made sure that they experienced the presence of God on a regular basis.

They learned how to worship God with others their age.

My wife would lead the weekly Church prayer meeting. She asked them to help her, so they learnt how to lead others in prayer and move in the power of the Holy Spirit.

Their Christian School would take the senior students to a major youth conference every year where most students had an encounter with God. Our own youth groups had similar types encounters with guest speakers. God would come with power. As a result, their passion for God grew and overflowed.

We also helped them to discover their God destiny for their lives and helped them step into it.

That's what we did, and it worked!

We do understand that not everybody has had that same

opportunity or experience.

Many leaders have children that aren't walking with God.

My response is always the same. Pray the prayer of agreement with one other person.

If you don't have a spouse, find a mentor or somebody who you can agree in prayer with every day.

Pray for your children each day. Don't pray what you think they should become but ask God to align them with their God destiny for their lives.

This prayer works.

**4. Physical Health**

One of the greatest challenges facing the western church is obesity. Most Christian leaders are free from worldly addictions like alcohol, smoking, drugs, gambling, possessions and the love of money but have replaced the need for those things with eating. So much so that the level of obesity in Christian churches is now an epidemic.

Along with being overweight comes a myriad of extra health challenges.

I've only ever heard one preacher speak about this before. He was very bold. He challenged us to change the prayer healing cycle. He said stop coming to the altar for prayer for healing if you are not willing to change your eating habits.

God does not want us to live this way. He wants us to take care of our temple.

Years ago, we chose to change out diet to a healthy lifestyle. So, we went and got help from a "Path to Thriving" health coach. She taught us that the biggest mistake most people make when trying to eat a healthy diet is that they remove all the wrong things that taste good from their diet without replacing them with a healthy alternative. This is the challenge with junk food and sugar addiction. We got rid of the soda drinks and the fast food. We were also taught that if any food package has more than four additives in it, then it's not healthy food.

As a result, our taste buds changed. We no longer desire that sort of food or drink with sugar in it.

In fact, removing junk food and processed sugar from our diet and food with a lot of additives was one of the best things we've ever done. We make our own green smoothie each day. We now eat a lot more fruit and vegetables that are straight from the farm without chemicals. We have learned to eat sweet alternatives that are healthy.

Paul says in 1 Corinthians 6:19-20-

> *Do you not know that your bodies are temples of the Holy Spirit, who is in you, whom you have received from God? You are not your own; you were bought at*

*a price. Therefore, honor God with your bodies.*

If our body is the temple of God, then we need to take care of our temple the body.

As well as diet, our body needs exercise every day.

Our goal is to exercise each day. The key is to raise your heart rate even if it's just for 5 minutes. So, we try to at least do one of these each day - bike ride, swim, run stairs or fast walk.

We have turned our walk into a prayer walk each day. So not only are we exercising we are also praying in agreement together as we walk. This has become a wonderful spiritual discipline that we enjoy practising.

You can too!

This is an important way to have longevity in your life.

Decide today to choose to live a healthy lifestyle. Maybe you will need help like we did to break out of old life patterns with our food. There were things that we thought were healthy that weren't.

Get some help from a health coach or a nutritionist.

## 5. Mental Health

Mental health is one of the greatest challenges facing western society. There are more people on medication for depression, anxiety, and a myriad of other issues than ever before.

What is even more concerning, surveys of pastors who are discouraged or depressed far exceed the national average.

In 2009, a survey[5] of protestant clergy in Canada showed that 20 percent of respondents had been diagnosed with an emotional condition; specifically, 16 percent said they had been diagnosed with depression. "This is double the Health Canada findings which states that approximately eight percent of Canadian adults will experience major depression in their lives.

A 2014 LifeWay[6] study among pastors in the U.S. found that these numbers didn't change in the time that transpired between the two studies. LifeWay's study indicated more than one in five pastors have personally struggled with mental illness of some kind.

What is the answer?

The Bible is very clear that as Christians we need to learn how to renew our minds into thinking God's thoughts.

Romans 12:2 says-

> *Don't conform any longer to the pattern of this world but be transformed by the renewing of your mind.*

The word 'transformed' is only used twice in the New Testament. Both times it refers to changing our mindsets.

If you don't change your mindset, when you come under pressure and things go wrong, you will revert to your old default coping mechanism.

You have to learn how to renew your mind.
Be careful what you watch and listen to. Most of the news, movies and social media will not help you.

The truth is that we all have the seed of sin in us. So, it's easy to become negative, critical, discouraged and even want to give up.

So, you need to wash your minds in the word of God every day. I use the daily discipline of Bible reading plan and I journal key points that God speaks to me from what I've read.

Learn to ask Him questions and listen for His voice. This will change the way you pray, and your perspective on your circumstances. It also greatly benefits your mental health.
Kenneth Copeland[7] says,

> *One word from God will change your life forever.*

Learn how to 'restore your soul'.
Long before David was king, he learned to do this. When he was fleeing for his life because he was being pursued by king

Saul who was wanting to kill him, David learns how to speak to his soul.

In Psalms 103:1 David speaks directly to himself-

*Praise the Lord, my soul; all my inmost being, praise His holy name.*

He is speaking to his own soul. Come on soul 'Praise the Lord'.

He learned the key to changing his thinking and restoring his soul was to speak to his soul.

More than telling his soul to praise God, he also learned the power of decreeing how good God was during all his pain and problems.

In Psalms 103:2 he speaks to his soul again. Again, he says-

*Praise the Lord, my soul,*

But this time he also tells himself to

*forget not all his benefits.*

He then goes on to list them and declare them all.

He says in Psalms 103:3-5 that he-

> *forgives all your sins*
> *and heals all your diseases,*
> *who redeems your life from the pit and crowns you*
> *with love and compassion,*
> *who satisfies your desires with good things*
> *so that your youth is renewed like the eagle's.*

He then reminds himself in verse 6 that-

> *The Lord works righteousness and justice for all the oppressed.*

That's you and me. Especially when we are experiencing pushback to our steps of faith by being oppressed and resisted by the devil.

He then goes on to remind himself how good God is to us all in verse 8–13,-

> *The Lord is compassionate and gracious, slow to anger, abounding in love.*
> *He will not always accuse, nor will he harbor his anger forever.*
> *He does not treat us as our sins deserve or repay us according to our iniquities.*
> *For as high as the heavens are above the earth, so great is his love for those who fear him;*
> *as far as the east is from the west, so far has he removed our transgressions from us.*

*As a father has compassion on his children, so
the Lord has compassion on those who fear him.*

In the process he encouraged himself in the Lord. He learned how to restore his soul.

We must do the same. This is how to live in good mental health.

| Action Points | My Response | Date |

## 2. Dealing with Obstacles and Discouragement

All leaders must cross the bridge of hardship and opposition. Accept it!

It comes with the 'Call of God'. Just cross that bridge now.

2 Corinthians 6:4-6 says-

> ..*as servants of God we commend ourselves in every way: in great endurance; in troubles, hardships and distresses; in beatings, imprisonments and riots; in hard work, sleepless nights and hunger; in purity, understanding, patience and kindness; in the Holy Spirit and in sincere love; in truthful speech and in the power of God.*

### 1. Learn to Overcome

The greatest challenge with the teaching on the favour and blessing of God is that many Christian leaders don't believe that God is in hardship.

But Jesus said just the reverse.

He addresses his disciples in John 16:33

> *In this world you will have TROUBLE.*

Yes!

Opposition and trouble come with the call of God!

In fact, it is a great compliment to you. It means that you're on the right track.

If you didn't have pushback from the enemy, then you wouldn't be making any impact or advancing the Kingdom.

But it is important to also remember that Jesus is the God of victory!

John 16:33 goes on to say.

> But TAKE HEART, I have OVERCOME the world.

It is so important for us to learn how to live in victory.

You're not a victim, you are a victor.

Victory is found in Jesus. He defeated hell and death and now is sitting on the right hand of the father with all things under his feet.

Paul says in Ephesians 1:18 that we must-

> know the hope and our glorious and heritance and his incomparable great power for all of us who believe.

Ephesians 1:19-21 then says-

> *That power is the same as the mighty strength he exerted when he raised Christ from the dead and seated him at his right hand in the heavenly realms, far above all rule and authority, power and dominion, and had every name that is invoked, not only in the present age but also in the one to come.*

Another way to overcome obstacles and discouragement is to practice rejoicing.

Now before you react and say "Yes, I know".

It is one of the keys to overcoming opposition and hardship and fulfilling the call of God for your life.

The prophet Habakkuk amid everything going wrong declares in Habakkuk 3:18

> *Yet will I rejoice in the Lord.*

Instead of complaining "Where are you God?"
And "But you said."

I am sure you have never said to God, "Why are you allowing this to happen?"

The prophet Habakkuk had learnt a powerful key. It is the power of rejoicing.

Even though everything has gone wrong for him, and he had lost everything, he decreed in Habakkuk 3:16 NKJV-

> *Yet will I rejoice in the lord....*
> *I will joy in the god of my salvation!*
> *God the Lord is my strength.*

It is so important that you develop an attitude of gratitude. You must learn to be thankful.

So many Christians are discontent with their lives. Learn to be content and grateful each day.

Let's take it a step further. Make contentment and gratefulness your lifestyle.

You may need to change your mindset to do that.

The first step is to believe that God is a good father who loves you and only wants the best for you.

You will read more about this later in Section IV.

How? Paul says in Philippians 4:4 to learn to-

> *Rejoice in the Lord always.*

Paul knew you really needed to get this, so he said it again!

*I will say it again: REJOICE.*


Why is giving thanks so important?

It works!

And it will help you to finish well.


It was the key for Nelson Mandela when he was in prison for 23 years. God broke into his mindset. He came out of prison a completely different person. Instead of getting bitter he got better. He learnt forgiveness and overcoming bitterness.


Rejoicing and gratitude has great fruit. it overflows into other aspects of your life. One of which is inner peace.


## 2. A Peace Operating System

Paul taught in Philippians 4:5-6-

> *Let your gentleness be evident to all. The Lord is near. Do not be anxious about anything, but in every situation, with Thanksgiving, present your request to God. And the PEACE of GOD, which transcends all understanding, will guard your hearts and minds in Christ Jesus.*

The peace operating system must affect every part of your

life. From driving the car to standing in line in a supermarket through to waiting for the answer to that unanswered prayer.

Peace only comes from God. That's why the apostle Paul says that you cannot truly understand peace. It does not make intellectual sense.

But God will give it to you even in the most painful, stressful, overwhelming, and discouraging circumstances.

We need to clothe ourselves in peace every day.

See yourself putting on peace like you would put on a pair of socks or shirt. Make it part of your prayer preparation each day.

Paul says it this way in Ephesians 6:15-

> *Put on the shoes of the readiness of gospel of peace.*

Walking in peace is a spiritual discipline.
Some days you'll do better and others.

Make the decision to put on peace and live in peace every day.

**Action Points** | **My Response** | **Date**

## 3. Being Able to Re-Vision

As mentioned earlier the main question that I ask leaders who I meet is,

*Are you enjoying your ministry?*

Most of them look at me with a puzzled look on their face.
Enjoy ministry? They had never considered that.
Most leaders think that leadership and ministry had to be endured rather than being enjoyed.

Jesus said in Mark 2:22-

*No one pours NEW WINE into OLD WINESKINS*

In 2015 several Apostles from all over Australia gathered to pray about what God was saying to the church and what needs to change to move into a new wineskin.

We asked each other and God this question-

*What does this New Wineskin look like today?*

After two days and then again meeting three months later we came up with the answer...

*It does not look like any one model of ministry.*

There is no right or wrong way. It is okay to be different. You do not have copy other leaders' model of ministry.

Sadly, in Australia, most churches use exactly the same model of leadership.

But you need to be unique. You don't need to have a certain multi campus model or a purpose driven church. If a corporate leadership model is not you, then don't use it.

What you do need is a new wineskin.

The new wineskin is a whole 'NEW MINDSKIN.'

It's a whole new mindset of doing ministry.

It starts with God breaking into your mindset and giving you a whole new way of thinking.

The truth is we need to change the way we think and see and do ministry.

The good news is that there is a whole new range of resources now available on the new wineskin.

One of which is my last book "A Whole New Era"[8].

The whole idea of revision is to change the way we think and live our Christian life.

**Keys to Re-Vision**

Here are some keys to help you Re-Vison.

**1. Don't be in a Hurry**

Most young leaders are in a hurry in the development of the ministry. But the truth is God never seems to be in a hurry.

I've always said that trying to do God's will at the wrong time is just as damaging as not being in God's will at all.

First you must learn to wait. God never seems to be in a hurry. But the more patient you are in waiting for God to give you direction the easier it becomes.

**2. Be Radically Obedient**

Even though I talk in more depth about this in Section 5, where you will be able to see your Leadership Timeline, it is important for you to grow in obedience.

Decide now that when you do get Gods direction, you instantly and radically obey.

### 3. Power of Repentance

Most Christians don't understand the power and fruitfulness of repentance.

In Acts 2 and 3 when Peter was preaching after the day of Pentecost, he challenged the crowd to repent of their sins.

Acts 3:19 gives us the powerful secret that when you repent-

*Times of refreshing from presence of the Lord*

If you need refreshing from God, the best way for you to receive is to humble yourself and repent of any known or unknown sins. Ask Him to dig up any hardness in your heart. When you truly turn away from self-centred attitudes, mindsets, and behaviour he promises to send the power of the Holy Spirit to set you free and refresh you.

Jesus said in Matthew 5:8 –

*Blessed are the pure in heart, for they shall see God.*

This is what repentance does for you. It purifies your heart and draws you close to God. Then you recognise His voice clearly and easily.

This works so much better than a holiday, days off and trying to escape your discouragement or frustration by watching endless movies or emotionally eating.

## 4. Soft heart towards God

The next key is to make sure that your heart is always soft towards God. One of the ways to do this is to make sure you have a teachable heart.

Jesus said in Matthew 5:5-

*Blessed are the meek, for they will inherit the earth.*

Another word for meek is humble. When you are humble, you are teachable. I've always said I would rather have a teachable young leader then a gifted one who was not willing to listen or to receive instruction.

Why is it so important to be teachable and humble? Jesus promised that you inherit the earth - you inherit your ministry here and now.

## 5. Love wins

My wife Cheryl has a wonderful saying – Love wins.

When we were newly married and we would have some disagreements, she would say, "If you humble yourself apologise and respond in love regardless of whether you are right or wrong, love wins".

Paul declares this power of love in 1 Corinthians 13:8-

*Love never fails.*

The key to leadership is to do what John the Apostle said in 1 John 4:7 -

*Let us love one another, for love comes from God. Everyone who loves has been born of God and knows God.*

And then in 1 John 4:8

*God is love. Whoever lives in love lives in God, and God in them.*

This is the Jesus way. This is the way to re-vision into maturity in your leadership.

| Action Points | My Response | Date |

## 4. Intimacy with The Father

### 1. The Orphan Spirit

One of the major causes of pastors being discouraged is the feeling of isolation and not being able to draw support from other pastors who should be able to sympathise with their struggles. There is a competitive spirit amongst pastors.

In the same Lifeway study, I mentioned earlier, 80% of pastors admitted to being jealous of the success of other pastors.

This competitive spirit comes from the 'orphan heart' that runs rampant in the body of Christ. The saddest thing is that it comes from older leaders who are supposed to be an example to the younger emerging leaders. But instead, they are threatened by them. Instead of being fathers they are orphans.

I have discovered two things about the orphan spirit. Firstly, it is easily reproduced in the lives of those we mentor or choose to follow our example.

Second, I have found that those with the orphan heart are sterile. They are unable to reproduce spiritual sons and daughters.

Sadly, orphans do reproduce leaders. But only the type of leader that are insecure, competitive, and often abrasive in their leadership. Their example will reproduce in the next generation of leaders. They become just like them.

The real reason why they are like this is because they have not experienced the Father heart of God.

After 25 years of ministry leading with an orphan heart, I encountered God the Father.

A team of us travelled to Mozambique to visit Heidi Bakers ministry in Pemba.

She has an amazing ministry of impacting the poor with the love of Jesus Christ with signs wonders and miracles.

Their ministry compound is full of orphan children who attend their school.

Every Sunday they hold a church service at their base. During the service Heidi asks all the 'overseas' guests to come forward. Then they ask all the children to come forward and to pray for each adult.

I had two orphans praying for me. They didn't pray simple childlike prayers. They passionately interceded for me that I would experience God's father's heart. They asked the Father to bless me with His love.

Heidi Baker is never in a hurry.

After fifteen minutes I began to weep. Up until then I had thought that they were the orphans; now I realized they weren't the orphans – I was!

Then after 20 minutes of them praying intently for me I had a powerful supernatural experience. When you have a Father heart encounter with God, the supernatural opens to you. In the spirit, I looked up to the ceiling of the church and saw a piece of paper floating down from the ceiling to me.

I said out loud to God through my tears,

*What is that Father?*

In reply I heard almost audibly,

*These are your adoption papers. Welcome home, son!*

Something wonderful happened in my heart that day.

From that time forward everything in my life changed! I had encountered the 'Father heart' of God.

I experienced God in a whole new way.

The good news is that you can change too.

The classic example of this in the Bible is King David.

In 2 Samuel 15 we see that David didn't start well as a father.

He allowed his son Absalom to conspire to overthrow his kingdom for four years.

Absalom had an fully developed orphan heart.

2 Samuel 18:18 tells us that Absalom was only intent on building his own kingdom and not his father's kingdom. So much so that he built a monument to himself.

This is the ultimate example of a fully developed orphan heart.

He was so obsessed with himself that he was even prepared to kill his own father so he could become king of Israel. Thankfully that didn't happen.

Orphan hearts accuse, undermine, and even try to destroy true fathers.

While David had to initially run for his life, eventually Absalom was killed, and David remained king and Israel was saved.

Acts 13:22 tells us how God saw David-

> I have found David, son of Jesse, a man after my own heart: he will do everything I want him to do.

David had discovered the Father heart of God.

He desired above all things to please God more than anything else. Even though he wasn't a good father with his younger son Absalom, God knew David had the potential of growing into a great father because of the posture of his heart towards God.

Towards the end of David's life, we see something wonderful had happened. He grew into a great father.

In 1 Chronicles 22:5 we are told that by the time Solomon was of age David had become a true father. He had grown a mature father's heart.

> David said, "My son Solomon is young and inexperienced, and the house to be built for the Lord should be of great magnificence and fame and splendour in the sight of all the nations. Therefore, I will make preparations for it. So, David made extensive preparations before his death.'

This spirit of sonship is available to all of you. You can experience it too!

## 2. The Spirit of Sonship

There is an antidote to the orphan spirit. It is the spirit of sonship.

The good news is that you can have an encounter with God the father and be delivered from that orphan spirit. And in its place, you will receive the spirit of sonship.

It changes your operating system from being led by an orphan spirit of insecurity, discouragement, loneliness, and competitiveness to knowing you are a son of God.

God knows us intimately! And he wants us to know him intimately.

David declares this in Psalms 139:10 when he said-

> *You have searched me Lord and you know me. You know when I sit and when I rise. You perceive my thoughts from afar......"*

God wants us to know his Father's heart and to experience him intimately!

Paul says this in Romans 8:14-15-

> *For those who are led by the Spirit of God are the children of God.*
> *The Spirit you received does not make you slaves, so that you live in fear again;*
> *rather, the Spirit you received brought about your adoption to sonship.*
> *And by him we cry, "Abba, Father."*

You were always intended for Sonship.

Paul says in Ephesians 1:4-5

> *In love he predestined us for adoption to sonship through Jesus Christ, in accordance with his pleasure and will.*

This is God's ultimate plan for you!

God desired from the very beginning that all of humankind would be His sons and daughters!

This was not an afterthought or an additional extra. This was in the heart of our Father God before the foundation of the world. It is also in the heart of God the Father for you too.

Che Ahn sums this up well in the foreword[9] of my book The Father's Love-

> *The love Jesus has for us is the love the Father has for us. Most people spend their lives trying to meet their legitimate need for this incalculable love illegitimately — never knowing why their need isn't met. It is only in letting the Father love us and knowing the love that He has for us that we will be fulfilled and radically transformed. It is the true love of our true Father— the truest heals the hardest of hearts.*

Even Jesus experienced God the Father's love. At his baptism in the Jordan river, the Holy Spirit came on him and he was filled with the power of God.

But Luke 3:21-22 something else happened at the same time. Everyone person heard God's audible voice say,

> *This is my son who I love, in whom I am well pleased.*

Imagine how that made Jesus feel?

After I had my father-heart encounter in Mozambique, I realised that I no longer had to try and please God. Just like Jesus. God the father was already pleased with me his son.

In fact, there is nothing that you can do that will ever separate you from his love.

He says in Romans 8:38-39-

> *For I am convinced that neither death nor life, neither angels nor demons, neither the present nor the future, nor any powers, neither height nor depth, nor anything else in all creation, will be able to separate us from the love of God that is in Christ Jesus our Lord.*

Once we have this sonship transformation in our souls, we can begin to live like true sons and daughters of God.

You will find that your perspective on life and ministry will change greatly. You will not be as driven or feel the need for people's approval. You will understand that you don't need to compete with any other leader or pastor to be successful.

It's no longer about the size of your ministry or how effective you must be.

Why? Because you're already successful you're already accepted. You're already pleasing Father God.

We must see with the Father's eyes. This is important for two reasons.

If we don't see with God, the Father's eyes we won't comprehend how great his love is for us.

And there is another important reason, you need to begin to look at others through the eyes of the Father.

My experience has been that once I truly knew God as my Father and understood His father's love, I started to look at others with my 'Father's eyes.'

Interestingly you will find that you see others very differently.

He will enable you to see others the way He sees them. I can now discern whether somebody is acting as an orphan or son. If a leader is acting as an orphan, rather than reacting to what they are saying or doing I listen to what the Father would like me to tell them. As a result, I have had multiple opportunities to speak the love of the Father into hurting leaders' hearts.

I also found that when you look with your Father's eyes you become very patient with the process of other leaders encountering God the father.

It's a whole new way of leadership. What God has done for me he will also do for you.

If you would like to know more read my book "The Father's Love – An Encounter with the Love of the Father"[10].

It will help you encounter God the Father and receive the spirit of sonship. You'll be no longer an orphan leader but a son.

PART 2 – HOW TO FINISH WELL

**Action Points** | **My Response** | **Date**

## 5. Change to Kingdom Values

It's no longer your ministry. It's His ministry.

You are called to build the whole body of Christ not just your ministry or church.

I can always tell if someone has this new wineskin by the way they talk. If their focus is on their ministry or their church rather than the wider body of Christ, I know that they haven't changed into the new yet.

Years ago, I had a conversation with a dynamic leader in our city. He was speaking about organising a major citywide Christmas pageant event inspired by Robert Schuler's Glory of Christmas that was held annually at the Crystal Cathedral in Anaheim in California. At the time I was the leader of a monthly prayer breakfast gathering for the northern part of our city. After meeting weekly for prayer and monthly for breakfast for many years, we decided God wanted us to move from having relational unity to working together in strategic unity. In other words, we believed it was time that we could influence that region of the city together for the Kingdom of God.

I was very encouraged when I thought that this leader was planning a citywide Christmas event. So, I enthusiastically said to him that I would ask all the pastors in our northern city network to join with him and help organise the event. I explained how it would impact the city and bless the whole body of Christ by them working together in unity.

He was stunned and said no because he was going to do it with just his church as he would gain many new members.

His response was disappointing but not surprising. It was not the first time that I had experienced this orphan hearted independent mindset of leadership.

This is not a value of the Kingdom of God.

However, when you change to a kingdom mindset things will shift dramatically for the Kingdom of God.

Jesus says in Matthew 11:12-

> *And from the days of John the Baptist until now the kingdom of heaven suffers violence, and the violent take it by force.*

The Kingdom of God is always advancing, but when you work together to build the kingdom you will have even more spiritual force in your sphere of influence.

It is also important to know the battles that God has called you to fight. In this new wineskin you cannot fight every Kingdom battle. Narrow your focus to what God has told you to do. Don't be distracted.

When other needs or opportunities come your way, always ask yourself this question-

*Is this the cause God has called me to fight?*

Typically, a leader is confronted with many 'God causes' but you must ask yourself-

*Is this MY God cause?*

In addition to this, the Apostolic office brings a whole new level of warfare.

I used to think that this was what Paul calls 'the marks of an Apostle', but now I don't think that way.

Yes, there are greater obstacles and there is greater opposition, but you have a 'breaker anointing' to break you out of that opposition.

Sometimes you only break through these obstacles through prayer and fasting. So, warfare prayer and fasting must be part of your kingdom values.

The key is to realise that there is more anointing and impact in a city when leaders work together rather than doing it yourself.

Isaiah 65:8 (NASB) reinforces this-

> As the new wine is found in the cluster....
> 'Do not destroy it, for there is benefit in it,'
> So I will act on behalf of My servants.

In other words, there is more power of the Holy Spirit released to impact a city or region for the Kingdom of God when you work together in unity using God's strategy.

We have proved this Kingdom principle many times over our decades in ministry.

One great example of this was when our citywide pastor's network was approached by a local city councillor. He was a Christian and was very concerned at the high level of domestic violence as well as the large percentage of single parent families in his electorate. I drew his attention to the fact that churches in that area of the city were closing and there were no youth groups for the children of these families. He asked would we be willing to do something together as the body of Christ. We also recognised that it was time for us to start working together in strategic unity, we accepted his request.

We began to strategize together as leaders as we sought God's plan to bring healing and redemption to this area in our city.

God gave us a three-year strategy that was multi levelled. First, we mobilised intercessors from all the churches to start going to that area on a weekly basis and prayer walking the neighbourhoods and around the government run elementary school. A National Youth ministry had just come to our city and when they heard the need, they offered to start running an after-school youth group. The principal was more than happy to allow them to use the school property to do this. Then after a few months that same school principal asked us if our combined churches would run a parenting seminar at night at the school.

We had also decided to bless the community by organising a huge free breakfast community event on Australia Day (which is our equivalent to the 4th of July in the USA). We called it The Great Aussie BBQ. Not only did we have free food, but we also had games for the children and free giveaways and quality entertainment for the adults. We fed over 1300 people that morning. Even though this wasn't the main priority, suddenly people discovered that they were no longer alone and that Christians really cared for them.

Over those three years, the youth crime rate was affected, and the dangers of domestic violence were addressed, and a support network introduced. Even though this was not one of the objectives, two new churches were started in that area in our city.

The Kingdom of God manifested when all the church leaders

looked past their individual churches and focused on building our city together.

This principle not only works on a citywide level, but also for you personally. God wants to enlarge your thinking and spiritual insight beyond just focusing on your ministry.

I hear the Lord declaring Isaiah 54:2 over you-

> *Enlarge the place of your tent, stretch your tent curtains wide, do not hold back; lengthen your cords, strengthen your stakes. For you will spread out to the right and to the left;*

It's time to enlarge the place of your mindset (tent). You need to start thinking bigger and beyond what you have done so far.

If you do Isaiah 54:3 says that-

> *Your descendants will dispossess nations and settle in their desolate cities.*

What a promise to you as a leader. If you are prepared to take a step of faith and change your leadership mindset to kingdom values, then God promises that your next generation legacy will be so large and effective you will impact cities and even nations.

Isaiah 54:4 goes on to say-

*Do not be afraid; you will not be put to shame.*

It's time for you to change your ministry and leadership mindsets. You have nothing to fear.

| Action Points | My Response | Date |

## 6. New Spiritual Disciplines

Life is so fast paced. As leaders you need to learn the power of not being in a hurry and feeling stressed. You need to pace yourself like a long-distance runner.

So, what are some new wineskin spiritual disciplines that you can add to your Christian life?

### 1. Fasted Lifestyle

My wife and I have been connected to Lou Engle since 1990. Lou mobilizes people over all over the world to fast and pray for specific prayer projects.

In partnership with Lou, we had the honour of leading The Call Australia in 2004. The Call was a National Day of Prayer and Fasting. It was preceded by 40 days of fasting. Over the years we have led many other prayer and fasting events as well as practising prayer and fasting as a spiritual discipline in our lives for as long as I can remember.

Recently the Lord began to speak to us about not only fasting when there was a specific need but to make fasting a lifestyle.

What does that mean? Rather than targeting prayer projects

or specific periods of fasting, we felt God encouraging us to fast each day of the year.

We did that by eating one less meal a day and permanently eliminating specific things from our diet.

The result of this lifestyle meant that we were continually in a prayer focus. It radically increased our level of spiritual insight and authority. So, we didn't need to be convinced that this spiritual discipline works.

We're not telling everybody to do this, however if you wish to add to your spiritual disciplines this is a good place to start.

## 2. Unhurrying your life and Solitude

God has called us to be at true to ourselves in Him. The challenge is there's so many expectations on us as leaders as well as the business of life and so many distractions whether it be demands of ministry, interruptions, even distractions in our own prayer time.

One of the keys to help reduce distractions interrupting my time with God is reading the word of God out loud. Especially the book of Psalms. I find that it seems to silence all the other voices in my head and I'm able to begin to focus on God and what I need to pray about.

Peter Scazzero[11] in his must-read book 'Emotionally Healthy Spiritually' says-

*It takes time (to slow down your life). I slowed down the pace of my life considerably from working six days a week (and about 70 hours). … this led me quite naturally to the classic Christian disciplines of silence and solitude.*

Silence is escaping from noises and sounds and solitude is being alone without human contact.

He goes on to say that silence and solitude are-

*so foundational to emotional healthy spirituality.*

Silence and solitude are not new spiritual disciplines. Moses, David, and Jesus practiced being aligned with God in silent prayer.

Mark 1:25 tells us that-

*Very early in the morning, while it was still dark, Jesus got up, left the house, and went off to a solitary place, where he prayed.*

And again, in Luke 5:16-

*But Jesus often withdrew to lonely places and prayed.*

In fact, all great men and women of faith have all practiced silence and solitude.

But it's even a greater challenge today for you.

As Peter Scazzero says-

> *With the hectic pace of our lives, the incessant noise of television, radio, computers, music, and our overloaded schedules, it is no wonder the ancient path of silence and solitude is lost to most believers in the West.'*

It will take practice and discipline to slow down your life. And even more practice to be quiet with God alone and meditate and pray in silence.

One of the keys to spending time with God in silence and solitude is listening. When most people pray, they spend most of their time speaking to God. But that's only part of what prayer is. Prayer is also learning how to listen to what God has to say to you. You can't hear someone speaking to you if you are talking. So, you have to learn to stop talking when you pray and just spend time listening to what the Father has to say to you.

Try it! It will transform your life.

## 3. The Power of Journaling

One of the keys to practising rest, silence, solitude and reading the Word is the spiritual discipline of journaling.

I have now been journaling each day for over 15 years. It has radically changed my relationship with God and the level of revelation from God's Word.

Initially we were taught to use a simple acronym called S.O.A.P when we started journaling. It involves a simple four step approach to reading the Word of God and responding to it. I began to use a Bible reading plan that would enable me to read all of the Word of God in one year and in fact you get to read the New Testament twice in my Bible reading plan.

But instead of just reading the Word, we were taught how to interact with is each day's readings.

S – Scripture. Choose one scripture verse that has speaks to you as you read and write it down.

O – Observation. As you read, what was one key observation that impacted or spoke to you?

A – Application. Write down how you can apply that in your life today.

P - Pray. Ask God to help you make that observation an application a reality in your life and through you that day.

You might think that might take a lot of time, that is not the case. Part of this discipline is to limit those four steps to just one page of your journal.

This new spiritual discipline of mine also radically impacted others. Many members of our congregation commented that my preaching had become a lot more powerful. There was no great secret to how this happened.

I just began to preach by unpacking principles that God had highlighted to me as I journaled his Word.

Not only did my journaling result in a preaching series but eventually formed the basis of notes to my first and subsequent books.

This is just the beginning point.

As I mentioned above. One of the most important aspects to spending time with God is learning to listen in silence to what God has to say to you.

You will discover that this will become watershed moments and guideposts for your life. So, make sure you journal what He says to you.

### 4. Cultivate the Spirit of Restfulness

Rest! Most people don't understand what true rest is.

Yet the Bible talks very clearly about the need for every one of us to rest.

In Genesis, God rested on the 7th day.

Genesis 2:2-3 says-

> *By the seventh day God had finished the work he had been doing; so on the seventh day he rested from all his work.*
> *Then God blessed the seventh day and made it holy, because on it he rested from all the work of creating that he had done.*

And He challenged us as his creation to do the same. Even making it one of the 10 laws or commandments that he gave Moses.

In Exodus 20:7-10 God commanded us to

> *Remember the Sabbath day by keeping it holy.*
> *Six days you shall labor and do all your work,*
> *but the seventh day is a sabbath to the Lord your God.*

When I sit down with leaders for the first time I ask them a number of questions including 'Do you have a day of rest each week'?

While many of them say they have a day off not many of them truly stop and rest the way the Bible instructs us to.

What is the Sabbath Rest?

The term Sabbath means to "Stop"!

God said one day a week you should stop!

In Hebrews 4:9 it says-

> There remains a Sabbath Rest for the people of God.

Most Christians never discover what this means let alone practice it.

Earlier I shared a Lifeway Study[12] asking pastors about their mental health. It goes on to say-

> *The majority of pastors surveyed said their contracts allowed them to take two days off a week, but most do not utilize those two days.*
>
> *Respondents work an average of 50 hours per week, with nearly 25 percent working more than 55 hours a week.*
>
> *Most ministers (80 percent) also indicated they feel guilty if people see them taking time off during the week.*

The Sabbath rest is more than taking a day off.

As mentioned, on my pastor's day off I use to do all the chores

that had been waiting for a week for me to do including organising housework and caring for the garden and swimming pool. And even going grocery shopping with my wife. None of those things are bad in themselves and sometimes that change in task does cause us to relax and restore our souls. But that's not what the Sabbath Rest is all about.

The majority of Jews in Israel today still practice the Sabbath. They understand the need to have a day of rest. In fact, they are incredibly enthusiastic about beginning that Sabbath rest. It is more than a cultural experience. It's a spiritual experience.

We have often been in Israel on a Friday leading up to start of the Sabbath at dusk. There is a genuine excitement on Friday afternoon leading up to dusk when the Sabbath begins. Everybody is happy.

That's why they greet with each other with 'Shabbat Shalom'. They are about to enter the blessing of a day of rest with God.

Hebrews 4:11 says-

*Therefore, make EVERY EFFORT to enter that REST.*

Why is this so important?

Even though most Christians don't practice Sabbath, the reason why we should is because God says to do it.

As well as that, the greatest symptom of the Spirit of the Age is restlessness.

Restlessness is the opposite to rest.

That's why the writer to the Hebrews told us in Hebrews 4 to make "Every effort to REST well".

The Hebrew word for Sabbath is 'Shabbat' or 'Stop'. What does stopping look like for you?

God wanted all humankind to stop for one day a week!

Not just to stop and do nothing but to use that day to cherish each other and God.

In fact, another meaning of the word Shabbat is 'Cherish'.

It is more than a day a week. It is spiritual discipline of restfulness that comes from abiding with God.

Here's some helpful hints in practicing the Sabbath.

You need to be intentional. You need to plan when and how to stop. It requires discipline and self-control to say no to good things and stop for a day.

People ask us what do you do on the Sabbath?

The answer is easy. We pray, read, talk, love and hang out with our family and above all rest.

Our first Israel experience of Shabbat was on Friday afternoon when people were excitedly going home to prepare for REST.

Shabbat begins with a special meal. While the Jews focus on God, there is a Christian version of the Shabbat meal. Then the focus is on Jesus. We use communion at the start of the meal, and we invite him to be the centre of our time together. We remember that he is the true bread of life.

All the family gathers. They stop and give thanks to God. It is joyful fellowship.

The next day in Jerusalem the roads are empty in the morning. No one is driving. The only movement you see is people later in the morning walking to synagogue to worship. After worship is over families often go to the parks and eat lunch and enjoy each other company.

We were blessed to experience how refreshing it was and how much joy people had practising the Sabbath.

Yes, we believe that God wants us to have a 'rest lifestyle'. Not just one day a week but every day.

It will have a major effect on the way you live the rest of your week.

John Mark Comer[13] says it this way-

*People who keep the Sabbath live all 7 days differently.*

Practicing Shabbat changes your lifestyle.

It is one of our weekly Spiritual Disciplines. While it is still a work in progress, it is helping us to finish well.

It will also help you to finish well!

**5. Power of Mentoring**

This is one of the most powerful disciplines. This is how you can have a Godly legacy and impact the next generation through intentional mentoring.

We all need to find trusted mentors. Not just friends in ministry but those mature trusted mentors who can help you to become spiritually and emotionally healthy.

Unfortunately, when you say mentoring many leaders think you're speaking about accountability.

Most leaders know the history of abuse in the Discipleship movement in the 1980s so typically people are reluctant to even explore the possibilities of what this may look like for them.

The challenge for most leaders is that an older form of mentoring has been the only example we have had. There has been confusion of understanding between discipleship, mentoring and fathering that has not helped. Most leaders would still refer to mentoring as discipleship.

But 'apostolic fathering' is a development from both.

Mentoring typically requires those being mentored as Paul says in 1 Corinthians 11:1 to

> *follow my example as I follow Christ.*

I teach that the Bible explores 3 levels of mentoring in the life of a leader.

We all need the first level of discipleship.

In fact, in Matthew 28:19-20 Jesus instructs us in the Great Commission to go into all the world and

> *make disciples of all nations.*

So, we all should obey the Lord's Commission and systematically disciple new believers.

Again, the best form of discipleship is by example.

The second level of mentoring in the Bible is between us and our peers.

What does this look like? It means that you actively seek out your peers for fellowship, encouragement and even accountability.

Yes, even asking others to help you to build on your strengths and address the inconsistencies in your leadership and life.

This takes honesty, courage, and transparency. But when you allow God to begin to break into areas of your life that only he knows about, your maturity and strength will multiply greatly.

I believe there is a need for another level of mentoring, in our leadership journey – by those in front of us in the form of a spiritual father speaking into our lives. This is the intentional fathering of spiritual sons and daughters. It must be systematic. By that I mean on a frequent basis in a formal setting so there can be continuity of input, accountability and reinforcing of 'new wineskin' thinking.

The most important distinction of apostolic fathering from the traditional concept of mentoring and discipleship is that it is 'next generational.' It involves the fathering of each person's unique destiny by a person who has a father's heart. Fathering is done intentionally and systematically. It builds, encourages, equips & then releases son and daughters into their destiny to transform the lives of others and then reproduce themselves again and again in the generation following them!

| Action Points | My Response | Date |

# Part 3 – Your Leadership Timeline

## Your Leadership Timeline

You need a God perspective for longevity in your leadership. Every leader develops in their leadership.
But do you know where you are on your leadership timeline?

Robert J Clinton's Book - The Making of a Leader says that God develops a leader over a lifetime.
He studied all the leaders in the Bible & 500 Leaders in Church History over a 15-year time frame.

At Fuller Seminary in Pasadena USA, as a young pastor, I had the honour to join his class called 'Leadership Emergence Patterns'. It was only for senior pastors and midterm missionaries. I wasn't one of those, but God gave me favour and I was allowed to join the class.

Clinton teaches all leaders have a Leadership Timeline. Not only were we taught the different stages or phases of our leadership emergence, but also, we were shown how to determine where we were on that Leadership Timeline.

This is an opportunity for you to discover your own Leadership Timeline. You are encouraged to spend extra time discovering exactly where you in your leadership development on the Timeline.

John Maxwell[14] in his book "Deveoping the Leader within You" defines leadership as 'Influence'.

The truth is that we are all leaders because we all influence someone whether it's a little or a lot.

# 1. The Phases of Leadership Development

There are 6 phases in every leader's Leadership Timeline

**Phase I - Sovereign Foundations**

This level is the starting point for every person whether you are a natural leader or not.

It is even before you experience being born again. It consists of those unique characteristics that you were born with and includes your personality and natural talents.

These include the different natural gifts in Romans 12:6-8

> *We have different gifts, according to the grace given to each of us. If your gift is prophesying, then prophesy in accordance with your faith; if it is serving, then serve; if it is teaching, then teach; if it is to encourage, then give encouragement; if it is giving, then give generously; if it is to lead, do it diligently; if it is to show mercy, do it cheerfully.*

This is before your experience of any Spiritual Gifts in 1 Corinthians 12 that come with the baptism of the Holy Spirit.

Later these gifts correlate with Spiritual Gifts after we are filled with the Holy Spirit.

Some examples are, those who are always passionate about sharing the gospel and excel in the gift of evangelism. Or those who have a sharp intuition excel in the gift of prophecy.

In addition, as Romans 8:28 says, God uses all your good and bad life experiences to build character in you, so you can be used by God.

**Phase II - Inner-Life Growth- Discipleship**

This level is where you discover God's call on your life. In the process you have begun your informal leadership training.

The major development task in Phase II is the identification of leadership potential and the formation of character.

It is when you begin your discipleship and Christian formation journey, the Bible tells us that Christ will be formed in you (Galatians 4:19).

The emerging leader learns the importance of praying and hearing God. You discover your call from God and what your destiny looks like. Re-read Section 1 of this book if you are still unsure of your God destiny or can't articulate it clearly.

It is also the phase where your integrity, obedience and character are tested.

Your integrity is the most important asset that you will have outside of your salvation. Unfortunately, many leaders fail in the integrity and character test. And you will be tested. It's not necessarily the enemy but God allowing you to grow through these challenges and the test of your character.

Many emerging leaders run from hardship. Often leaders are so discouraged that they give up and no longer follow the call of God on their lives. But Robert Clinton teaches us in his book that these character tests are all part of a boundary phase that every leader must grow through as they move from one leadership phase to the next phase of their timeline.

Learning to endure and radically obey God no matter what, is one of the most important lessons a leader in this phase can learn. All emerging leaders are meant to learn how to radically obey God and not give up regardless of the circumstances.

Not only do we need to know God's will, we need to obey his direction. The quicker you respond in your obedience and trust him no matter how difficult your situation is, the more the Lord will trust you and build your life as a leader.

In Luke 7 Jesus had an encounter with a Roman centurion soldier whose servant was dying. Jesus agreed to go and heal the centurion's servant. But the soldier just sent Jesus a message saying you don't need to come. Instead, he told Jesus in Luke 7:7-8

*But say the word and my servant will be healed. For I*

*am a man under authority.*

This Roman centurion was not only a leader, but he understood the power of God's promise and authority over the circumstances surrounding him. We need to learn this principle as a leader too!

The Bible tells us that Jesus was amazed by this soldier's response to him.

So much so that he said in Luke 7:9-

> I tell you; I have not found such great faith even in Israel.

Why was this such great faith? Because the centurion understood the power of a being under authority and acting on to the direction of those in authority over us.

These are the essential keys of discipleship. This is how Christ is formed in us. This is how you grow in your early phase of leadership.

**Phase III - Ministry Maturing**

This phase involves your informal training and your spiritual growth. Ministry becomes the primary focus in life.

The major development task of Phase III is 2 fold-

1. Initial identification of gifts and skills and the increasing use of them in order to develop a growing effective ministry.
2. The development of an experiential understanding of the body of Christ. This will include many relationship lessons – both negative and positive. [15]

I had such a passion and hunger for more of God when I first became a Christian. I knew right from the outset that I had been called by God into the ministry. Not only was I on fire for God, but I was also hungry to grow and learn. But I was in a traditional denomination, and I was surrounded by young people who weren't as on fire for God as I was, so I learned very quickly that I had to feed myself.

I read Christian testimonies and all the books on revival that I could get my hands on. Each week I would finish at least one or two books. I was the Christian bookstore's best customer. I was continually listening to as much teaching from great men of God as I could. I simply couldn't get enough input. What was God doing? He was training me and causing me to grow spiritually.

As I would read about the great men and women of faith in revival history, my heart would burn.

I would see visions of me standing before large crowds of people preaching the gospel with people responding for salvation healing and deliverance.

As a result of all this I realised that I needed to change my focus in life. I no longer wanted to be a chartered accountant or a millionaire. I had no longer had a choice. I had to go into full time ministry.

At the same time my pastors and leaders could see the call of God on my life and started to give me more leadership responsibility. I began to preach at first only occasionally but then at least once a month. I started to lead a Bible study on the power of the Holy Spirit where I learned how to pray for the sick and cast out demons... yes that was happening in our Bible study! I was out evangelising on the streets. The fire of the Holy Spirit was moving inside me to spill out onto others.

I realised that I didn't want to do anything else with my life except serve Jesus full time for the rest of my life.

So that led me into this Phase III of exploring full time ministry options and learning how to use my spiritual gifts. This is part of this phase of the maturing of your ministry call.

The wonderful thing is that it is organic not orchestrated, unpaid and unscripted.

The emerging leader begins to rise up in spiritual authority and kingdom influence.

Ministry activity or fruitfulness is not the focus of Phases I, II, and III.

God is working primarily in the leader, not through him or her. [16]

He wants to teach you that you minister out of who you are.

The next two phases are essential for you to have longevity in ministry.

**Phase IV - Life Maturing**

The Life Maturing phase of a leader's development involves a powerful synergy unleashed as ministry coincides with gifts. The leader Identifies their gift mix, and they begin to use them with power resulting in great fruitfulness.

During this time the leader will focus on what to do and not what to do in ministry.

This will result in mature faithfulness.

Isolation, crises, destiny experiences take on new significance for a leader….[17]

The principle that 'ministry flows out of being' has new significance.

Most leaders who have been in ministry a long time are here at this stage.

It is here that God helps you identify your gift mix and used with power. This will move you to mature fruitfulness. You know that you are becoming mature in your life in Him when you-

- Minister from who you ARE in Him
- Many life lessons will zero in on your relationships with other people and inadequacies in your personal life.
- You gain a sense of priorities concerning the best use of gifts and you understand that learning what not to do is just as important as learning what to do.
- Your understanding of God is being developed through encounters with Him.
- The leader's character mellows and matures.
- Communion with God and Intimacy becomes foundational in your life.
- It is now more important to you than success in ministry.

The major development task of Phase IV is the deepening of the leader's experiential understanding of Christ which increases their spiritual authority. [18]


Sadly, most leaders and emerging ministers don't progress through, let alone past this phase.


They don't ever move into convergence.

But convergence is essential to finish well.

## Phase V - Convergence

Convergence happens in a leader's life when their-

> *Character, experience in ministry, formal and informal training, mentoring and your spiritual life converge and overflows at the same time.*

In convergence the leader is moved into a role that matches their giftedness and frees up the leader to do the best that they have to offer.[19]

Life Maturing and Ministry Maturing peak together during this phase.

Everything in your life converges and overflows at the same time resulting in the Lord dramatically increasing your effectiveness as a leader.

Your spiritual authority and influence overflows. It results in great impact and great effectiveness for the Kingdom of God in your city region and even nation.

Many other leaders begin to recognise what God is doing in you and through you. This results in the leader becoming widely accepted and recognised by the whole Body of Christ.

One of the most recognisable leaders I know in convergence in Australia is David Balestri. As well as having his own business mentoring ministry and being one of the pastors of his local church, David leads nationally as the apostle of the Australian Coalition of Apostolic Leaders (ACAL). He is also the apostolic advisor to the Australian Prophetic Council. His business equipping mantle is strong, yet he also functions powerfully in the church mountain. He is widely regarded right across the whole body of Christ as being one of the emerging apostolic fathers in this nation. One of the main manifestations of his leadership convergence is the fact that he is now able to bless the whole body of Christ and not just his ministry or denomination or one mountain of influence. There is a manifestation of blessing that flows over every sphere that he has contact with and leads. This is what convergence looks like.

To get to the place of convergence the power of God converges all life experiences, hardships, successes, authority, anointing, and emotional maturity with your leadership gift to bless and build up the whole body of Christ.

In convergence it's no longer about you and your ministry. It's about building the whole Kingdom of God.

Most importantly, your main emphasis is on being in Him[20].

Sadly, many leaders don't ever experience convergence. There are many reasons for this including the lack of the leader's personal development. Some reasons are hard to understand. Sometimes it is enough for you to know that God calls you to function in your current phase of leadership.

I do believe one of the main reasons is because they have an old wineskin of success and ministry. Sadly, the need for recognition by their peers withholds the overflow of the new wine of the Holy Spirit. As a result, they don't see generationally or develop a next generation focus and don't ever experiencing legacy in leadership.

The major developmental task for a leader in Phase V, Convergence is guiding the leader into maximum ministry effectiveness.

Convergence is not a goal. It is the by-product.

It so important in your leadership development.

It is essential in you finishing well as a leader.

If you are willing to decide today that you will allow God to build your leadership, you enter into the fullness of your convergence in your leadership development. In the process you will build the whole body of Christ and finish well.

## Phase VI - Afterglow or Celebration

This is what longevity in leadership and finishing well looks like.

Afterglow happens when a leader's ministry has been

influential and impacting of the body of Christ over an extended period. This is when leaders are celebrated by whole body of Christ. Typically, they are no longer leading ministries but still active in building the Kingdom of God and enjoy the afterglow of effective ministry. Their focus is no longer 'my ministry' focus but fathering next generational 5-fold apostles, prophets, evangelists, pastors, and teachers.

I have seen a great example of a leader recently in Afterglow. Fergus McIntyre is a grandfather of the prophetic movement in Australia and New Zealand. Just recently he spoke at the at the Australian Council of Prophets. He leaks sage wisdom. When he speaks people hang on every word. Not just what he says but who He is in God. His exhortation to the body of Christ in Australia was simple but profound.

After no longer travelling as itinerant prophet, he has sat at the feet of Jesus for two years. He exhorted us to learn to sit with Jesus and "allow God to get at us."
His words were weighty. He overflowed with the presence of Jesus.

There are many other examples of fathers with a next generation mindset. Billy Graham and Oral Roberts are two of the best examples that I know of leaders finishing well. They were still ministering powerfully and effectively to the next generation even though they were no longer able to be as active in ministry as they used to be.

Longevity is always a powerful symptom of a very healthy organisation.

Billy Graham's reputation is remarkable. He won more people to Christ in the 20th century than any other person. But what most people don't know is how remarkable the Billy Graham association was and still is. Billy Graham had a long term relationship with all his key leaders.

Each one of the key leaders in the Billy Graham association had all been with him for over 40 years.

Even when Billy Graham had health issues in his 80s and 90s, he still gave direction to the ministry and would host many next generation leaders in his home. The Billy Graham organisation trained and helped facilitate thousands of evangelists around the world over many decades. Billy Graham did not stop. He kept influencing for the Kingdom of God during his afterglow years of leadership.

In the last few years of his life Oral Roberts decided to start meeting with national and international leaders at his home every week. He would encourage them to go further than he had gone, mentor them, bless them, and then financially sow into each of them. My spiritual father Che Ann had the honour of visiting Oral Roberts as one of those leaders. He said that meeting was one of the most significant meetings of his life. Oral Roberts went out of his way to bless all the next generational leaders before he went to be with the Lord.

Perhaps the most contemporary example of a leader transitioning leadership to the next generation and finishing well was Reinhard Bonnke.

Bonnke is not only famous for the millions of people won to Christ during his life, he is also one of the few leaders who raised up a next generation successor. He handed over the ministry while he was still at the peak of his leadership. His mentoring of Daniel Kalinda was so effective that the leadership transition was seamless. This is how leaders in Phase VI lead and live.

We have many examples in Australia of leaders in this phase of their leadership timeline. A few wonderful leaders like Margaret Court, Col Stringer, Jenny Haggar, Peter Vacca and Andrew Evans all understand the power of building the body of Christ by raising up next generation leaders.

Afterglow is the sustained overflow of their effective ministry.
They function as a father and mother of new generation leaders.
They function in the 5-Fold with maturity and unity.

Their sole focus is building the Kingdom of God through the whole Body of Christ.

We pray that there be even more leaders with this level of maturity and heart for the next generation in our near future.

Most leaders never experience true Afterglow. Be determined to be a leader that does finish well like this.

**Action Points** | **My Response** | **Date**

## 2. The Generalised Timeline

The following describes the important generalised development tasks from God and suggested responses from leaders that are necessary in each of the seven phases of each leader's timeline.

### Development Tasks for The Generalised Timeline

| Phase | God's Developmental Tasks | Leader Response |
|---|---|---|
| Sovereign Foundations | Laying of foundations in the life including leadership potential. | Respond positively. Take advantage of these foundations. |
| Inner-Life Growth | Identification of leadership potential. Formation of basal leadership. Character through testing. | Respond positively to testing. Be prepared for the expansion after test. |
| Ministry Maturing | Initial identification of gifts and skills for ministry release for leader. Increasing use of skills and develop gifts. Teaching relationship lessons. Unfolds ministry philosophy. | Recognition of gifts and skills. Take steps to use those gifts and skills. Learn & use lessons of submission and authority. Catch the Vision. |
| Life Maturing | Deepen understanding of God. Develop intimacy with God, not success. Focus on relationship with God as primary responsibility not success. | Respond positively to deepening processing. Deepen Communion. Recognize ministry flows from being. |
| Convergence | Guidance of leader into role and place of maximum contribution. | Trust and rest and wait. Make decisions based on convergence ideas. |
| Afterglow | Bring glory to God for a life-time. | Honor God's faithfulness. |

| Action Points | My Response | Date |

## 3. Your Leadership Timeline

Now is the time for you to discover where you are on your own individual timeline. It's always good to be able to put dates against each phase on your timeline. You might also want to include significant occasions, changes, and milestones in your timeline. Most importantly try to remember some of the boundary phase experiences that you went through before you moved from one phase of leadership to the next.

Further information is available from Robert Clinton's book "The Making of a Leader"[21].

In Robert Clinton's leadership course, we were all required to draw our own timeline and plot where we thought we were in a particular phase in that timeline.

Interestingly many of us who had been leaders of ministries all felt that we were in a boundary phase between two different levels of leadership.

Typically, things don't happen very quickly during those times. So much so that some leaders feel like that they have even failed or are no longer able to keep going.

Clinton says-

> While it is true that each individual leader's timeline is unique, it is also true that there are similarities in all leader's timelines.

Clinton goes on to say-

> The comparative study of over 250 leaders in the bible and in history have identified common features that relate to the personal growth of a leader[22]

When we drew our own leadership timeline, we were able to see that God was indeed still guiding us and in the process of moving us from one phase of leadership to the next.

This was one of the greatest gifts that was given to me as a young leader. When you understand where you are in the leadership development process, it gives you great perspective and an understanding of how God is leading you and developing your leadership.

This is why this leadership timeline exercise is so important for you to do.

It is time for you reproduce the timeline below and begin to re-examine the definitions of each phase of leadership. Then ask God to show you exactly where you are on your leadership timeline. Remember there is no right or wrong answer. Resist the urge to want to be in a leadership phase beyond where you are. Because this will be of no benefit to you now and in the future.

**Draw your Leadership Timeline**

I encourage you to draw your own Leadership timeline. Spend the next 20 to 30 minutes filling in your leadership timeline.

Use a large blank piece of paper to reproduce the graph below and begin to fill it in. Draw the actual line with the six phases of your leadership.

Make sure you include all your significant life developments including the date and what took place in each of your leadership phases as you have moved to your current phase.

Locate where you are now.

Remember - Each new Phase has boundary phases in between. Include changes / character tests / and mentors.

You will find this process very encouraging, and you will be able to see the big picture and where you are exactly in your leadership development.

| Phase I | Phase II | Phase III | Phase IV | Phase V | Phase VI |
|---|---|---|---|---|---|
| Sovereign Foundations | Inner-Life Growth | Ministry Maturing | Life Maturing | Convergence | Afterglow / Celebration |

| I___ | II___ | III___ | IV___ | V___ | VI___ |
|---|---|---|---|---|---|

| Action Points | My Response | Date |
| --- | --- | --- |

# Part 4 – Your Next Generation Legacy

## Your Next Generation Legacy

God is the God of generations. He is the God of Abraham, Isaac and Jacob. He wants us to think generationally too. God tells us in Psalms 145:4 that

*One generation commends your works to another;*
*they tell of your mighty acts.*

His plan was always for multiple generations and not just one leader. Luke 1:50 says-

*His mercy extends to those who fear him, from generation to generation*

More than that we have a responsibility to raise up the next generation of leaders.

As Psalms 78:5-7 says-

*He decreed statutes for Jacob and established the law in Israel, which he commanded our ancestors to teach their children, so the next generation would know them, even the children yet to be born, and they in turn would tell their children. Then they would put their trust in God.*

## 1. Your Ceiling Their Floor

David understood the need to teach and raise up the next generation.

He says in Psalms 71:18-

*Even when I'm old and grey, do not forsake me, my God, till I declare your power to the next generation, your mighty acts to all who are to come.*


As leaders we also have the same assignment from God. This is part of how we finish well.


Psalms 22:30-31 says it this way-

*Future generations will be told about the Lord. They will proclaim his righteousness declaring to a people yet unborn.*


Proverbs 13:22 says-

*A good man leaves an inheritance for his children's children.*

A good father does this for his natural children. Now do it for your spiritual children.

As Ephesians 2:20 says, we must be-

> built on the foundation of the apostles and prophets.

Most define modern day apostles and prophets as spiritual fathers and mothers.

Bill Johnson says according to Ephesians 2:19-20, fathers and mothers are foundational. Your ceiling is their floor!

You were always meant to be the floor. The foundations. Not the top for everybody to look at and admire. But the floor that the next generation will stand on and build on top of.

The body of Christ needs you to become the spiritual fathers and mothers who will do this!

However, it won't just happen. You must be intentional.

We are told in Psalms 78:5 to-

> Teach (mentor) your children.

We need to teach both our natural children and our spiritual children.

The good news is that you are never too old to start.

Psalms 71:18 says-

*Even when I'm old and grey I will declare your power to the next generation.*

| Action Points | My Response | Date |
| --- | --- | --- |

## 2. Next Generation Legacy

Generations are dependent on your decisions today.

This is best seen in the story of Ruth and Boaz, her kinsman redeemer husband.

Boaz's obedience and righteous decision impacted the future of the nation of Israel.

The genealogy in Matthew 1:5-6 tells us that Ruth and Boaz had a son, his name was Obed. He grew up and got married and had a son. His name was Jesse. And Jesse grew and got married and had many sons. One of them was David, the greatest king of Israel.

Generations are dependent on your decisions today!

Proverbs 4:1 says-

> *Listen my sons, to a father's instructions. Pay attention to gain an understanding."*

In verse 4 Solomon speaks of his father's teaching

> *Then he taught me.*

He goes on to say in verses 4-6-

> *Take hold of my words with all your heart.*
> *Keep my commands - you will live.*
> *Get wisdom. Get understanding.*
> *Do you not forsake wisdom and she will protect you.*
> *Love her and she will watch over you.*

More than just the next generation, generations are depending on your leadership legacy.

In Deuteronomy 3:26–28 God told Moses he would not enter the land. But he saw it!

When Moses realised that he would not enter in, he knew he had to commission, Joshua (the next generation) to lead his people.

So, it's one thing to be an example and to leave a legacy for the next generation, it's another thing to commission them and send them forth with authority and power.

Normally, when you appoint a successor, they take over from you and lead whatever way they see fit. However, if you have this next generation mindset, you will have already mentored and made provision for your successor to step into your shoes and they will carry on your DNA of leadership.

In Galatians 4:6-7 the apostle Paul says that-

*Because you are his sons, God sent the Spirit of his Son into our hearts, the Spirit who calls out, "Abba, Father." So, you are no longer a slave, but God's child; and since you are his child, God has made you also an heir.*

There is a progression here. We first need to experience God's Father's heart. Through that encounter we enter the true spirit of Sonship. God's plan was for you to be more than his son, he also wanted you to raise up heirs. The truth is you can't be an heir unless you raise up your sons.

Success in ministry is no longer defined by size or fame.

| Action Points | My Response | Date |

## 3. Success with a Successor

You will not be a Success until you raise up a Successor. That's what the word Successor[23] means-

*To come next after another in office or position, especially to inherit sovereignty, rank, or title: to follow after another in order.*

But we just don't want someone to take over from us, we want them to make much greater impact than we have done. We desire for them to step up into a greater level of Glory that our generation ever experienced.

Even though we won't necessarily see it, we can help prepare them for it.

The leadership model has been training up leaders and then sending them out to do their own ministry. It's like throwing a child in the deep end of a swimming pool and telling them to swim without any swimming lessons. But that's not the way of the kingdom.

Mature loving fathers and mothers want our natural children

to succeed in life. Good wishes alone, won't cause them to do that.

We need to help prepare them for their future after we've gone. to make sure before they begin that they will succeed. So we do everything we can to help prepare them for their future leadership and success.

David did this for Solomon.

As we read earlier, 1 Chronicles 22:5 tells us that David realises that Solomon was-

> *young and inexperienced and the house to be built for the Lord should be of great magnificence and fame and splendour in the sight of all the nations. Therefore, I will make preparations for it.*

So, David made extensive preparations before his death.

David understood that Solomon's leadership needed to be bigger than his. But it was beyond Solomon's capacity at that time. So, David helped prepare him so he would be able to do it in the future.

David was mentoring his next generation successor.

Notice he just didn't say 'You can do it. I believe in you'.

It sounds nice but it's not what your successor needs.

What you are really saying is

*You are responsible now. Go and do it yourself.*

That's not the attitude God wants you to have towards your successor.

Why? Because there's no preparation for them to receive their next-generation legacy.

Thankfully, David did understand the need not only to train future leaders, but also to help them now to step into the fullness of their future, leadership, authority, and mantle.

David's maturity and understanding of his role was very significant and speaks to us today.

Why is this so important?

You're making sure that the next generation, leaders, don't just replace you and are successful, but you are ensuring that they will surpass you in your leadership influence, effectiveness, and transformation.

Leadership transition has always been portrayed as leaders passing the baton, like runners in a relay race. But my sense is that God desires that this generation of fathers to go further than that with our next generation emerging, fathers and mothers.

We must father them. Teach them how to lead as fathers and mothers.

Be brave enough to let them lead while we are watching. In other words you give them the opportunity to lead while you're still alive. This doesn't mean that you resign and let them take over. You give them enough room to lead so you facilitate them, so you make sure they succeed in their future leadership function. So much so that they go much further than you could.

You are setting them up to springboard them forward.
We indeed want them to go further than we have gone.

This is the heart of next generation leadership.

PART 4 - YOUR NEXT GENERATION LEGACY

**Action Points** | **My Response** | **Date**

## 4. It's Your Turn Now

Jesus took twelve and he trained them intensely for three years.

He wasn't just the discipling them. He was preparing them for their future role to build the Kingdom of God.

But he didn't just train them. He also then told them to go ahead and do it.

He told them it was their turn.

In Luke 9:1-2 Jesus gathers the disciples together and sent them out!

> He gave them power and authority to drive out all demons and to cure diseases, and he sent them out to proclaim the Kingdom of God and to heal the sick.

And they went.

Luke 9:6 tells us-

> *So, they set out and went from village to village, proclaiming the good news and healing people*

*everywhere.*

We see the sequel to this in Luke 9:10-17. They returned to Jesus and reported to him all they had done. I'm sure Jesus would have rejoiced with them and encouraged them to keep being bold and exercising their faith and authority.

Jesus and the disciples left to go to Bethsaida, but the crowds followed them. Jesus was happy to see the crowds and spent time teaching them about the Kingdom of God and healing the sick.

Luke 9:12 tells us that when it was getting late in the afternoon the disciples said to Jesus to send the crowd away so they could find food and accommodation.

Jesus' response was profound. In Luke 9:13 he said

*You give them something to eat!*

Why? Jesus, was telling them-

*It is your turn now!*

He had already discipled them over three years, giving them power and authority over demons and disease, and sent them out preach the Kingdom of God.

He was saying-

*I've already sent you, it is your turn, now go and do it!*

God is saying to you today too 'It is your turn now'.

**The Holy Spirit will enable you to raise up next generation leaders.**

Once you say 'Yes' to your next generation legacy, the Holy Spirit will enable you to raise up next generation leaders.

I used to say,

*If you don't quit, you win.*

But winning is no longer about you. Not anymore!

The Holy Spirit teaches us in all truth.

So if you ask God for help when you are struggling, the teacher, the Holy Spirit, will come along side you and will help you finish well.

We saw this powerfully demonstrated to us recently.

One of our granddaughters recently ran her first cross-country race. Even though she was only six years old, the race was for 750 metres. Which was far too long for such a little child.

Unfortunately, she had trouble keeping up with the other runners, then she made a mistake. She stopped running. She started to walk. By that time, she was so discouraged she looked like she was going to stop altogether.

But then a teacher came along side Lucy and took her hand and ran alongside her and helped her finish the race as they ran together.

This is a wonderful picture of the Holy Spirit coming along side you and helping you finish your race.

Leadership is not about titles, position, or success. It's about influencing other people's lives for God and for their best life.

Which leads us to the need for you to be willing to send out others to fulfil their calling.

This is the main thing that apostles and prophets are required to do. You need to send leaders out, not keep them to build your own ministry.

Most fathers, and mothers in the faith, understand the need to equip the emerging generation. But we need to do more than equip them. Ephesians 4:11-12 says we also must release them. It's of no use training and equipping somebody if you never release them to go. They must fulfil their destiny and lead their generation and the generation to come.

Jesus sent out his twelve apostles after he had discipled them for three years.

In Luke 9:1-6 Jesus, called the 12 together, and he gave them-

> *power and authority to drive out all demons and to cure diseases and he sent them out.*

After teaching, equipping, and raising up the next generation, give them the power and authority to go to their own generation and build the Kingdom of God.

This is exactly what Jesus' apostles did. Luke 9:6 says-

> *So, they set out and went from village to village proclaiming, the good news and healing people everywhere.*

The book of Acts records how the next generation of disciples who were filled with the power of the Holy Spirit impacted the world then and generations after generations since.

It also includes you.

Why? You need to follow Jesus' example with your next generation sons and daughters.

This is the best way to have next generation legacy.

It is your turn now!

| Action Points | My Response | Date |

# The Final Word – You Will Finish Well

## The Final Word – You Will Finish Well

Long distance running still fascinates me. Especially marathons. It is not so much about who wins. What attracts me the most is the high level of endurance that it takes to finish the race.

As I said in my Introduction, the analogy for us as leaders is very powerful.

My prayer is that you have caught not only the need to run the race with endurance, but also how to successfully finish your race of leadership and life with next generation legacy.

I love celebrating longevity. Especially celebrating leaders who have led consistently and maturely with a father's heart over decades.

Longevity with legacy in life speaks very powerfully.

My own mother and father-in-law were married for 71 years. A remarkable achievement.

I love celebrating couples who have been married a long time. Not just because of the length of time that they have faithfully been committed to each other, but also it speaks so very loudly to young couples today. We live in a disposable western society. When things get tough people often give up on their relationships. There is very little understanding on how to have longevity in marriages. This is also true in ministry today.

When someone has been married a long time, I always thank them publicly and tell them that their longevity speaks so loudly to all of us. We want to follow their example.

Perhaps some of the saddest things I've experienced is when we hear of couples who fail in both in their marriage and ministry. They don't finish well.

At the outset of our marriage over 40 years ago, my wife and I made the decision before God that divorce was never an option. We believed then, and still believe today, that if you walk in the love of God and are prepared to be committed to keep building your marriage, your marriage will last a lifetime.

This same principle is also true for the longevity of your leadership and your next generational legacy.

Most leaders know of others who have not finished their race of leadership and ministry. God does not want you to be like Philippides and be another statistic. Ministry was never meant to be endured so you collapse before or even at the finish line.

Like Paul in 2 Timothy 4:7 God wants you to finish your race well. He does not want you to be another casualty.

I decree over you that-

> *You will fight the good fight, you will finish the race, you will keep the faith.* (Paraphrase mine)

If you have interacted with God and allowed Him to transform you as you have read this book and got to this final word, I can say with confidence that you have been called by God to run the race of leadership with longevity and will finish well.

But there is another reason for you to finish well. You have a leadership legacy. And the next generation needs for you not only to give them a good example, but also teach them how to run the race and finish well too.

As I have already said in this book, the decisions that you and I make today impact generations to come.

I encourage you to take this challenge very seriously. Let there be a holy determination in your heart never to quit and to run your race with perseverance.

Remember it's not how you start your race; it's how you finish it.

My prayer is that because of your interaction with God as you have read Longevity in Leadership - How to Run the Race and Finish Well, God has created a greater endurance in you.

You will not only have longevity in your leadership, but you will also finish your race of life with influence and legacy for the next generation that is following your example.

I have every confidence in you. You will finish well!

The final word must be from the writer to the Hebrews.
I decree over you that you will indeed do what Hebrews 12:1-3 says-

> *Therefore, since we are surrounded by such a great cloud of witnesses, let us throw off everything that hinders and the sin that so easily entangles. And let us run with perseverance the race marked out for us, fixing our eyes on Jesus, the pioneer and perfecter of faith. For the joy set before him he endured the*

*cross, scorning its shame, and sat down at the right hand of the throne of God. Consider him who endured such opposition from sinners, so that you will not grow weary and lose heart.*

| Action Points | My Response | Date |

# Endnotes

1    Pheidippides (Greek: Φειδιππίδης, "Son of Pheídippos") or Philippides (Φιλιππίδης) is the central figure in the story that inspired two moderns sporting events, the marathon race and the Spartathlon. Pheidippides is said to have run from Marathon to Athens to deliver news of the victory of the battle of Marathon
Wikipedia - Created by: Jimmy Wales; Larry Sanger; www.wikipedia.org

2    Merriam-Webster's Dictionary of English Usage (MWDEU) published by Merriam-Webster, Inc., of Springfield, Massachusetts. Reprint edition (1994).

3    John Wimber at Anaheim Vineyard' Prophetic Conference – January 1991
Anaheim Vineyard. John Wimber was the founder of the Association of Vineyard Churches, also known as the Vineyard Movement.

4    Merriam-Webster's Dictionary of English Usage (MWDEU) published by Merriam-Webster, Inc., of Springfield, Massachusetts. Reprint edition (1994).

5    "Health Canada - 2009, a survey of protestant clergy in Canada". Published in www.churchleaders.com

6    https://research.lifeway.com/wp-content/uploads/2014/09/

Acute-Mental-Illness-and-Christian-Faith-Research-Report-1.pdf

7   Kenneth Copeland – Believer's Voice of Victory, Fort Worth, Texas.

8   "A Whole New Era" by R. Bruce Lindley 1st Edition published by the author. Copyright 2020.

9   Che Ahn's Foreword in "The Father's Love – An Encounter with the Love of the Father" by R. Bruce Lindley Copyright 2016. Published by A.R.C. Global PO Box 4393, Helensvale B.C. QLD 4212, Australia

10   "The Father's Love – An Encounter with the Love of the Father" by R. Bruce Lindley Copyright 2016. Published by A.R.C. Global PO Box 4393, Helensvale B.C. QLD 4212, Australia

11   Peter Scazzero - Emotionally Healthy Spirituality - Updated edition. Zondervan 2017

12   Life Way Study – "Why are Pastors Depressed?" - 23rd September 2019 www.churchleaders.com

13   "The Ruthless Elimination of Hurry" – John Mark Comer. Crown Publishing Group, Copyright 2019

14   John Maxwell, "Deveoping the Leader within You' - Thomas Nelson 1993

15   Leadership Development Theory. Comparative Studies Among High Level Christian Leaders by James Robert Clinton. Doctor of Philosophy Dissertation, School of World Mission, Fuller Theological Seminary, November 1988. p300

16   ibid p300

17   ibid p301

18  ibid p302

19  ibid p302

20  See Colossians 2:6-7 - "So then, just as you received Christ Jesus as Lord, continue to live your lives in him, rooted and built up in him, strengthened in the faith as you were taught, and overflowing with thankfulness."

21  The Making of a Leader: Recognising the Lessons and Stages of Leadership Development by Robert Clinton Second edition Nav Press 2012. Copyright 1998, 2012 by J. Robert Clinton All rights reserved used with permission Tyndale House Publishers Inc.

22  Leadership Development Theory. Comparative Studies Among High Level Christian Leaders by James Robert Clinton. Doctor of Philosophy Dissertation, School of World Mission, Fuller Theological Seminary, November 1988. p296

23  Merriam-Webster's Dictionary of English Usage (MWDEU) published by Merriam-Webster, Inc., of Springfield, Massachusetts. Reprint edition (1994).

www.ingramcontent.com/pod-product-compliance
Lightning Source LLC
Chambersburg PA
CBHW051429290426
44109CB00016B/1484